Best Kept HR Secrets

*400 Most Powerful Tips For Thriving at Work,
Making Yourself Indispensable &
Attaining Outrageous Success
in Human Resources*

Alan Collins

Success in HR Publishing
Chicago, Illinois USA

Dedicated to my son, Bryan.

Fifty percent of the proceeds of this book will
go to the Bryan A. Collins Memorial Scholarship Program
which provides scholarships to deserving, high potential
minority students who excel in academics and in
service to others. I encourage you to join me in
supporting this truly worthwhile cause at
www.BryanCollinsScholarship.org.

WHAT THIS BOOK IS ALL ABOUT

In *Best Kept HR Secrets*, you have in your hands a compilation of the world's best advice for thriving at work, making yourself indispensable and attaining outrageous success in Human Resources.

Just like my first book, *Unwritten HR Rules*, this book cuts to the chase. It won't waste your time being politically correct, sugarcoating the truth or concealing the realities of what it takes to win big in HR. Instead...

This is proven, no B.S. wisdom that practically no one else in HR will sit down and tell you about.

No matter where you are in your HR career, a few minutes spent with this book will make your brain explode with aha's and possibilities. **It contains over 400 short tips, best practices, ideas, discoveries, confessions, and brutal truths on practically ANY subject related to your success in Human Resources.**

Many of these lessons have been learned the hard way through my own successes, personal screw-ups and painful mistakes. However, it also features the advice and wisdom of many other prominent leaders - both inside and outside of the HR field.

So, it will save you a lot of angst. This is the book I wish I had throughout my HR career.

Time and money used to be our planet's most precious commodities. Not anymore. Today, I believe our most valuable resources are *life experiences* because no one has the time to share theirs with you...especially if you're in HR.

Just about every HR leader I know works with one eye on their job and another eye on the invisible ax that could fall and whack that job at any time. Most are constantly challenged to prove their value, meet aggressive deadlines, attend endless meetings, come up with innovative HR programs and achieve enormous expectations that rise every day. That's just a fact of life. However, as a result, it's tough for most of the truly outstanding folks in our profession to carve out time to coach and share their HR career experiences with you. So, consider this book their written surrogate.

This book will help you work smarter, faster, bolder, with bigger goals and a better appreciation for your own potential.

Now, a confession: I never intended to publish this information. But, here's why I changed my mind.

Ten years ago on a plane coming back from a business meeting, I started scribbling down a few pages of personal insights about HR for a presentation to my HR team. I thought a short collection of discoveries that influenced my own life and career in HR might be a good change of pace at the end of the meeting. To my surprise, the ten minutes I spent sharing this information with the team was the best part of that session. Their reaction told me that there was (and continues to be) a voracious hunger for human resources advice and lessons from those who have willing to share wisdom from their own personal career journeys.

After that meeting, I kept all those old notes and decided to add to them over time. I bought a thin black spiral bound notebook to capture my thoughts and began carrying it with me everywhere. I'd always been a bit of pack rat and collector, so I started collecting and compiling nuggets of wisdom relevant to attaining success in HR. **Anytime I'd hear an inspiring piece of advice, instructive truth or an insightful personal story from an HR colleague, boss, mentor, HR thought leader or a great leader....I'd capture it and jot it down in this notebook.** I did this off and on for years. As time passed, this notebook got beat-up and most of the pages became yellowed, torn, coffee-stained and dog-eared.

A year ago I misplaced this darn thing and thought I had lost it forever. Everywhere I looked, I couldn't find it. During the time it was missing, I became frustrated because I realized how priceless this information had become. This amazing collection of HR advice had evolved into my main "go-to-resource" that used over and over again whenever I had an HR problem, needed some inspiration or just a kick in the butt.

Fortunately, one day while moving from one office which was cluttered to a nicer, new office (which would soon be just as cluttered as the old one)....I came across an old box buried in a closet that I hadn't seen daylight in months. In this box, I found my black binder with all my notes...intact.

So, I decided then and there to turn it into this book. One, so that others in HR could gain the same benefits I had gained. And, two so that I would never, ever lose it again.

Here's how to squeeze the most juice from these pages.

This book is for the busy, overworked HR professional who doesn't have time to read a book from cover to cover. My guess is that covers 98.5% of the HR population. With that in mind, here are the ways you can get the most value from this book:

#1: Use it for inspiration and to help you solve your own tough HR career dilemmas.

It's not practical to attempt to put all these insights into action at once. You'll go crazy. So, flip to a page at random, and see what's in store for you there. Put your finger on any sentence or two. If you're not using the idea that you touch, consider starting. If you are using that idea, that's great...now, flip to another page. Go page by page. Or take out the highlighter and mark up the pages or even put x's through those things that you don't agree with. The key is to make this yours. I've even added a couple of blank pages at the end of this book for you to add your own reflections.

#2: Have it available to you at all times as your portable coach.

Carry it with you when you travel. Have it on your nightstand. Keep it on your desk. Sometimes huge bells will go off in your head while reading through these nuggets. Use it to provide a jolt of inspiration or a whack on the rump when you need it.

Some of this you will want to move on immediately. Some of this you'll want to take some time to think through first, before acting.

#3: Share this with your HR staff. If

you're an HR leader, pass a copy of this book on to members of your team as part of their professional development. Encourage them to internalize, try out or discuss or debate these insights with you. Ask them what they agree with and what they don't. Find out what nuggets in this book inspire them or upset them. Either way I'm sure you and they will be positively enriched from the discussion and the experience.

Thank you in advance for investing your time in this book. I'm confident your returns will be infinite.

Enjoy and best regards,

Alan Collins

Alan Collins

400 Most Powerful Tips For Thriving at Work,
Making Yourself Indispensable &
Attaining Outrageous Success
in Human Resources

#1:
It's easy to impress your clients with your knowledge of HR...when you've impressed them with your knowledge of THEIR business -- *FIRST.*

#2:
You need an HR specialty.
Even if you're a generalist and jack of all trades, you need to be a MASTER OF ONE. It makes you unique, special and sets you apart from the rest of the pack.

#3:
The HR job you're in RIGHT NOW is the best launching pad for your career success.
Perform superbly in your current HR role and you've laid an awesome foundation for super success in HR. *So, if you don't feel you can win BIG where you are now, either resolve to step up your performance TODAY or move into a new HR role elsewhere! Not tomorrow, NOW!* While it's unlikely that one single job will make or break your career, a consistent track record of success does. And that track record goes through the job you're already in. Can some people succeed in HR by not demonstrating excellence in what they're doing right now? Sure. Some people win the lottery, too! But very few people achieve meaningful and lasting success without committing themselves to excellence in what they're doing right here, right now. Begin.

#4:
HR results matter a lot, but relationships matter more.

Performing and delivering results matter. They help you attract attention, recognition, rewards and promotions. But only up to a point. **When you reach the Human Resources leadership ranks, this perspective shifts radically. Results continue to be just as important, but relationships you build within the organization carry even greater weight.** Organizations are inherently social – they run on relationships. As you climb the ladder, you are expected to balance aggressiveness and drive with the ability to develop trusting and collaborative relationships with your peers. It is a cost of admission to the executive suite. Leaders work long hours together, often under stressful conditions, to achieve their goals. It stands to reason they want to surround themselves with team members they respect and with whom they have rapport.

#5:

Go first. Waiting for others to reach out to you creates success in waiting, not in building relationships.

#6:

If you're an HR leader, nothing will make you look better than a talented HR team. Hire people who are at least your equal or preferable a little bit better. Too many B and C players will ruin your department and your leadership reputation.

#7:

STAY CURRENT AND ON TOP OF YOUR HR GAME. JUST WHEN YOU THINK YOU'RE WINNING THE RAT RACE, ALONG COME FASTER RATS.

#8:

What others say about your HR reputation is 10 times more convincing than what you say -- even if you're 10 times more articulate.

#9:

Unless your boss knows you're great and so does her boss...and anyone else who could be your boss...advancing your HR career in your current organization will be nearly impossible.

#10:

Most super-successful HR folks have LOTS of projects in the pipeline -- any one of which could change the course of their career overnight. Check and add to your pipeline often.

#11:

If You Mess Up in HR, Fess Up. Fast!

If you screw up, confess and tell the whole truth. No blaming. No excuses. No CYA. Tell the truth to anyone you can fess up to: your boss, your people, your clients, the receptionist, the guy at the bar, your cat. Everyone. Do it on little things. Do it on big things. It doesn't matter. THEN, GET ON WITH YOUR LIFE, with a clear conscience.

#12:

Embrace & use the F-word often.
(Relax, F stands for feedback.)
Set up regular face-to-face meetings to clarify, dig deeper and decode any vague and confusing feedback you receive about your performance, your style or your approach in handling difficult situations. While it's ok to clarify it, don't debate it, argue about it or shut it off. Consider feedback a gift and when receiving it, the MOST appropriate response is:

"Thank you!"

#13 - #24:
Twelve Dirty Little Secrets For Landing Your Next HR Job

One: Your HR experience doesn't matter NEARLY as much as it used to.

The old rules were: Tell me what have you done? **The new rules are: Tell me what can you do?** This may seem unfair or even ridiculous. But the reality is hiring managers don't want to hear about everything you did way back when. They want to hear about everything you can do, to help them TODAY. Right here. Right now. Employers want HR people that are problem solvers. If you cannot clearly articulate how you contribute (directly or indirectly) to enhancing retention, reducing costs, improving revenues, and helping them become more competitive, you might as well stay at home.

Two: You CANNOT depend on a résumé to get an interview.

Forget spray and pray. Applying to every HR job in sight with the same, un-customized resume is a total, utter waste of time. Simply mass-mailing out hundreds of résumés and then sitting back and waiting for responses never worked. And today it's just consumes your time, your paper, your postage, and your emotional energy…with no payback.

Three: You can't rely on job fairs.

Years ago, job fairs were a fantastic way to hire highly qualified people. Today, job fairs have become thankless, confidence-crushing meat markets. Instead of spending money on dry cleaning and parking to attend a job fair, do this instead: contact employers one by one after you've done your homework re-searching their businesses and their problems.

Four: You shouldn't expect to hear back.

Unfortunately, this little courtesy has become as ancient as the horse and buggy. Expect many of your follow-up calls go unre-turned. People are just too swamped or don't care. Sure, that isn't an excuse. But, you combat this by continuing to network, interview, and research companies right up until the moment you have a firm HR job offer in your grubby little hands. Maybe even a little after.

Five: Your résumé is no longer a complete summary of your work experience.

Don't bother to list HR jobs more than 15 years old. They really don't matter that much. Instead, quantify your recent accom-plishments, emphasize your HR certifications and highlight your leadership capabilities. Also, your resume needs to be digital-friendly, easily uploadable, downloadable, and scannable (i.e., no bullets, boxes, boldface, unusual fonts, indenting). It should be rich in the "keywords" that recruiters and HR hiring manag-ers are looking for.

Six: You should forget resume-blasting services.

There are lots of vendors who would love to blast your resume out to a gazillion employers for a fee. Like #2 above, this is simply more spray and pray. Employers are buried with resumes already. Your unsolicited, un-customized resume is the last thing they want to see. Skip these services and conduct your own research, using search engines and LinkedIn. Then write to hiring managers directly with targeted overtures.

Seven: You must be web savvy.

Get comfortable with applying for jobs online and learn how to do research online. If all this is new to you, your public library is a good place to start. Oh, and have a professional-sounding e-mail address. It is also a great idea to go one step further and establish a strong online presence. Explore LinkedIn (get some stellar endorsements), Twitter, and Facebook. Become active in your field's social media sites. Consider building your own Web site (with a career-oriented blog, professional photo, and résumé).

Eight: Forget video resumes.

Imagine the hiring manager sitting at her desk swamped in re- sumes, cover letters, reference lists, portfolios, and unanswered emails from job applicants. What's her incentive to watch your video resume? There isn't one. Video resumes are a solution in search of a problem. Instead, craft a killer resume and get it out to hiring managers, along with a pithy "pain letter" that explicit- ly shows how your HR background makes you the perfect person to relieve their business' pain.

Nine: You must google-proof yourself.

One of the first things a potential employer will do is Google you. That means you need to find out if there's anything nega- tive about you online. If there is something bad, get it removed. If it's not easily removed, your best bet may be to "bury" it with more recent, more favorable information about you posted on- line through articles and blog posts…all authored by you.

Ten: Posting "I'm job hunting" messages on LinkedIn, Twitter, Facebook or HR job boards have little to no success.

I always feel bad for HR folks who I've never met who e-mail me on LinkedIn with a message that says, "I am seeking an HR job." I'm a total stranger to them. The odds of getting a HR job lead that way is about the same as you or I getting cut in on Oprah's will. If you're like me, you want to know the people you refer for job opportunities. And, if you're a job seeker, you're better off spending your time making one-on-one connections or following up by phone or in person with people you know already...or their referrals.

Eleven: If you're a seasoned HR executive, many interviewers, hiring managers, recruiters may be younger than you are.

If you've been in the HR field awhile, get used to it. Take your ego out of the equation. Treat them with respect and learn how to speak their language. Do not say "You remind me of my son/daughter," or "When I was your age..." They know you may mean well, but it's tacky.

Twelve: More than ever, it's all about who you know...AND who knows you.

This is the most critical point of all. Landing your HR dream job today is less a matter of applying for existing open positions and more about identifying needs potential employers have and demonstrating to them that you can address their problems. Fortunately, there are more networking venues (offline and online) than ever before. Successful HR job seekers get results through thoughtful, well-crafted letters, resumes, phone calls, and LinkedIn overtures — sent in response to posted job ads or sent to employers who don't currently have jobs posted but who may well have business needs anyway. They also do it through networking and through careful follow-up with the people they know and the new people they meet during their job search. "Hey, I need a job" is not a compelling pitch – but "I think I understand what you're up against, and would love to talk about solutions" very definitely is.

#25 - #28:
4 C's For Building Tremendous Credibility in Any HR Job

I used to give a presentation as part of a two-day orientation for our new hires in HR at Quaker Oats. There were 36 things that we'd tell them they needed to do in order to be successful. It included how you interview job candidates, coach, hold career discussions and do appraisals. As I would get up to conclude the training, I knew from past experience that it was impossible for them to remember every-thing. So I would wrap up by saying that their *credibility* and *reputation* were the most important currency in their HR jobs and that the following four things were crucial in building it:

The first is competence. Focus on being the best in your HR job — whether you're a generalist or in compensation or labor relations. Reach for the higher standard. This means focusing on the job you have, not on the job you want, and committing to grow your skills to become great at what you do.

The second is confidence. While it's great to ask questions to gather data in an employee investigation, your clients want to know what you think. Lea-dership is about having a point a view and sharing it. So you have to have enough confidence in yourself to regularly and unabashedly put your own perspectives and ideas on the table in tough situations.

The third is caring. No one individual can accomplish great things in large, complex organizations. Success requires collaboration. And at the end of the day, it's giving a darn and partnering with your clients and your colleagues and recog-nizing that it's the people around you are the ones who make you look good in your HR job.

The fourth are your connections. Your relationships are a require-ment for producing results beyond yourself. They expand your ability to get things done and allow you to produce things that you can't in isolation. They give meaning to our lives and provide a platform for extraordinary results. The more people you can influence the more power you have.

#29:

Brilliant HR pros know EXACTLY when and how to address their clients' needs:

- Sometimes your clients just want you to provide them with a step-by-step process to follow on their own. Provide it and step away.

- **Sometimes your clients want an ear. If so, just listen, hear them out, be their sounding board and they will feel well served.**

- Sometimes your clients just want you to check in with them, ask how they are and offer them some extra time and help.

- Sometimes your clients need your support and validation that what they are doing is right or that they're on the right track.

- Sometimes your clients don't want you to bother them at all. They want independence, so give them their space.

- **Sometimes your clients want to know that you're available 24/7 if they need to call you. Most of them may never call, but knowing they can is good enough.**

- Sometimes your clients want you to connect them to the right people: HR specialists, consultants, coaches, your colleagues or your boss. Provide them access to your network.

- Sometimes your clients want you to challenge them, ask more of them, instead of just being "supportive and available." Raise their bar, help them play a bigger game and they'll love you.

- Sometimes clients like to be surprised with gifts, cards and other items. Almost everyone likes to receive a surprise, just don't make it a bribe.

- **FINALLY...sometimes your clients won't follow your HR advice, no matter how terrific it is. Don't take this personally. Accept this reality and focus on EVERYONE ELSE.**

#30:
HR pessimists complain about the wind.
HR optimists expect it to change.
HR leaders simply adjust the sails.

#31:
Be authentic and be yourself.
Everyone else is taken.

#32:
Do HR work that truly inspires other people and helps your company succeed and career opportunities will chase you.

#33:
Never underestimate what you know. What may be common knowledge in HR to you may be a revelation of immense value to someone else.

#34:
HR leaders when faced with ambiguity and uncertainty keep in mind that in the land of the blind the ONE EYED MAN IS KING.

#35:

The Awesome Power of Mentors

A University of Virginia and Harvard study found that people with three mentors are more likely to get promoted than someone with fewer than three. They also perform better on the job, earn higher salaries and report more job and career satisfaction. This is true in HR as well. I've never found an exceptionally successful HR leader who cannot name a cadre of influential mentors who helped their careers along the way. **When selecting mentors, avoid those who belittle your HR ambitions. The poor ones do that. The great ones make you feel that, you too, can become great.**

#36:

Leave the words "human capital" in the textbooks, conference rooms and with the HR consultants. In real life, you can't treat people LIKE THEY'RE NUMBERS IN A POWERPOINT PRESENTATION or as "HUMAN CAPITAL" THAT CAN BE SOLD OFF LIKE A STOCK THAT'S IN FREE FALL. They're people, like you and me, with families, fears and aspirations for the future. And for most of their day, they choose to invest their time and energy in our organizations. Remind yourself each day that in Human Resources, your unique contribution to the organization's success is all about people, not objects.

#37:

Speak plainly. Drop the HR and OD jargon, psychobabble and buzzwords. State things so your grandmother can understand them.  Put a kibosh to the acronyms. Approach every HR presentation, every email, every discussion you have as an opportunity to show how brilliant you are using *your own words and language!* Imagine that your grandmother is listening to your message. Naturally, she is a very intelligent woman since she has a grandson or daughter like you in HR. Do you think she understands words like: organization effectiveness, intellectual capital, rightsizing, core competencies, bandwidth, *and the all-time favorite: being strategic.* Of course, she doesn't. And, how many other folks do you regularly talk to that might be in the same boat as your grandma?

#38:
Stop running the holiday party.

You don't have to be scrooge. But why should you be the social secretary all the time. As an HR professional, you have a real job with real deliverables. Let someone else handle it like Finance or Sales. It's their turn.

#39:
You will advance much farther in HR if you **trust people first**, rather than mistrust people first.

#40:
As an HR leader, if you're never disappointed, your expectations aren't high enough. Raise your standards and start EXPECTING MORE. You and your team will perform better when surrounded by higher expectations.

#41:
The fastest way to change results is to CHANGE THE PEOPLE producing them.

#42:
When your HR workload is taking priority over your family or taking care of yourself, you're not prioritizing or delegating enough.

#43:
If your company's culture doesn't allow you to bring your real, authentic self to work, you will be uncomfortable short-term and miserable long-term.

#44:

How to avoid becoming irrelevant in Human Resources. According to Dave Ulrich, there are six key HR leadership competencies you must have to thrive in today's economy. If you don't master them, you're Fred Flintstone in a George Jetson world. They are:

- **Being a credible activist**: Someone who can earn and maintain the trust of employees and managers, while taking strong and proactive business positions.

- **Being a business ally**: Someone who has a solid understanding of the business financials, strategies, and context and uses them to make better decisions.

- **Being a strategic architect**: Someone who can take the business' strategic story and translate it into HR practices and leadership behaviors.

- **Being an operational executor**: Someone who can ensure things happen on time, every time.

- **Being a talent manager and organization designer**: Someone who can shape HR practices that deliver talented people and capable organizations.

- **Being a change agent**: Someone who can make change happen and can help create new cultures, values and expectations.

Are these skills in your portfolio? If not, every day they aren't, you're falling farther and farther behind the rest of the pack.

#45:
The way to receive huge amounts of recognition and credit in HR is to GIVE AWAY as much of them as you possibly can.

#46:
Enthusiasm and passion will cover many of your deficiencies in HR.

#47:

The only two ways to get people to change fast is through inspiration or desperation...and the latter is often the MOST effective.

#48:

A crisis is a terrible thing to waste. People will band together and accomplish truly amazing feats when faced with a truly urgent situation and will make change happen in months, not years.

#49:
The HR leader's job is CHANGE. If you're not spearheading and guiding change, you're managing - not leading.

#50:

To achieve true greatness in HR, you don't have to aspire to the HR C-suite or make millions in base salary in a Fortune 100 company. Just define what greatness means for you and you've taken the single most empowering step you can take in your HR career. There is no ONE way to achieve greatness in HR except to find a way to spend your time doing what creates enjoyment in you and others. Do what you're good at and passionate about. And, don't think that the only way to progress is up. Just close your eyes and picture what would create the most personal fulfillment. Figure out all the details and then start working towards it. One. Step. At. A. Time.

#51:

Doing good HR work alone is not good enough. For one thing, no one knows what the heck you're doing in your office or cube if you're not telling them. So when you do good work, let people know. **It is NOT crazy to toot your own horn – it's crazy to think someone is going to take the trumpet out of your hands and do it for you.**

#52:

When wrestling with a tough HR problem, it helps to find a dark room and shut your eyes in order to see things more clearly.

#53
Three people that need to know your salary:
1. The IRS
2. Your spouse
3. The headhunter finding you a better job.

#54:

Don't make excellence the prisoner of perfection.

The quest for perfection will slow down your ability to get results throughout your HR career. Take action now and get it done. **Motion beats meditation!** He who goes from notion to motion fastest wins! Get on with it. Get it done. Get it out.

#55:
In HR, when one door closes another opens. Don't let anger over the closed door blind you to opportunities in the open one.

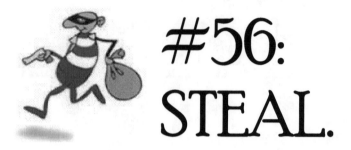

#56: STEAL.

Never Invent Mediocity When You Can Copy Genius.

Swipe BEST PRACTICES from any place and anywhere you can if it helps move your HR department, your HR career or your business FORWARD. Steal from other departments. Swipe from other divisions. Take from other firms. Be sure you give them credit - then add your own UNIQUE twist. If it's proven and it works, why not? BURY YOUR EGO. Creating new stuff from scratch always takes more time than you think and is highly overrated.

#57:
Giving great HR is about solving problems.
The day your clients stop bringing you their problems is the day you've stopped being effective. They've either lost confidence that you can help them or they've concluded that you don't care. Treat either case as a WAKE UP CALL.

#58:
A truly great HR leader searches for eagles, not turkeys, and then teaches them to fly in formation.

#59:
The 3 most important keys in managing your poor performing employees:
1. Clear expectations
2. Documentation
3. Feedback

#60:
You don't have to wait for great opportunities for your chance to do great things. SEIZE small everyday things and do them in a great way.

#61:

Never accept garbage in your HR department.

If your Human Resources function is to be credible, it cannot be where people go when they've failed everywhere else or can't find meaningful employment. Demand the absolute best and the brightest in your department, just like everyone else. Besides, after awhile, garbage stinks.

#62:

Cut the work before cutting the workers.

In tough times, eliminating unnecessary, redundant and low value work improves productivity. *Eliminating people doesn't.* Sure, cutting people looks great on the P&L. But you haven't really improved the organization's performance when 30 "survivors" are struggling to do the work that 50 FTE's used to do...and are suffering in silence and are so frustrated they're suicidal.

#63:

Don't create workarounds for BAD MANAGERS.

Expect them to behave like paid professional leaders. Don't give them hall passes to avoid giving performance reviews, providing developmental feedback or having candid career discussions with their people. Your job in HR is to help your company work in the best way possible. You shouldn't have to develop policies to make up for "managerial malpractice." If managers can't or won't manage effectively, follow the medical profession model and pull their "license" to manage anyone... forever!

#64:

Keep a note pad, pencil or blackberry on your bedside table. Great HR ideas or solutions sometimes strike at 3 AM.

#65:

Treat your full-time, permanent HR position as a temporary job disguised with benefits -- because in today's economy, it is.

#66:

In HR as in life, your supporters make you happy but it is your critics that make you better. An honest critic is your best friend.

#67:

You don't progress in HR based on how smart you are, but based on how many ACTIONS you take to succeed!

#68:

In recruiting and hiring, don't use cost per hire as your only success metric. It matters, but QUALITY OF HIRE IS FAR MORE IMPORTANT. After a period of time, the only thing people remember is how great your hire was, not how much he or she cost.

Nobody remembers how much Michael Jordan cost to sign. And those that do don't care, because he created billions and championships.

Nobody cares that John Gruden was paid $8 million to coach when he won the Super Bowl.

Michael Jordan will lift your team.

Tiger Woods (despite his indiscretions) will lift your golf tournament.

Angelina Jolie on the cover will sell more of your magazines.

The same is true of your superstars in Finance, IT, HR, Sales, Engineering, or Marketing. They will lift your organization and pay for themselves many times over.

#69:
Courageous HR folks are unafraid to take a stand and express their point of view. **Sometimes when you straddle the fence, you sit on a spike.**

#70:
WHEN PLANNING YOUR HR STRATEGY, DIG DEEP INTO YOUR TURNOVER NUMBERS. Losing the top performing 20% of your people is 5 times more hurtful to your organization than any other group. **It's not HOW MANY you're losing, it's WHO you're losing.**

#71:
"DON'T EXPECT OTHERS TO LISTEN TO YOUR HR ADVICE AND IGNORE YOUR EXAMPLE."
That's what a division CEO I reported to once told me. He went on to say: "As our HR leader, I expect you to be the conscience of the organization. Your ethical standards need to be higher than anyone else on my leadership team. *I know that doesn't seem fair, but if you can't accept that, then let's talk about finding you another job.* You cannot be credible and help me hold our leaders accountable for behaving ethically and fairly with their people…if you're not walking the talk yourself."

#72:
Always stand when greeting a visitor to your office. It shows respect.

#73:
In HR, every knock on your door, email, or call can potentially ruin your day…or be an opportunity that can make your career. Be prepared.

#74:

When you find an ideal HR job, don't sweat the pay. If you've got what it takes, your salary will soon reflect your value ~ if not where you are, then somewhere else.

#75:

When negotiating your salary, figure out what you want, then ask for 10% more...and you'll smoke out their best offer.

#76:

Moving up isn't always the best path. When you look up the HR career ladder of success you're likely to see 100-hour weeks, meeting overload, blackberries on night-stands, and no time for friends and family. If this isn't for you, take time to re-define and customize the ladder of success for yourself. *Don't feel that you must climb someone else's rungs.*

#77:

Office politics is about caring, not backstabbing. The people who are the most successful at office politics tend to be genuinely pretty cool and nice. Sure there's scum too, but they're in the minority. Office politics is about helping people to get what they want. This means you have to take the time to listen, figure out what someone cares about, and then think about how you can help him or her to get it. It does require having your ears open for when you can help. If you do this, you don't have to trample over people or manipulate them. Your genuine, authentic caring will inspire people to want to help you when you need it.

#78:
WATCH FOR BIG ORGANIZATION PROBLEMS. THEY DISGUISE BIG HR OPPORTUNITIES YOU CAN LEVERAGE TO ADVANCE YOUR CAREER.

#79:
Take the stairs when it's four flights or less.

#80:
Accept a breath mint if someone offers you one. Always. Always. Always.

#81:
Promoting your best performer to HR leader is often a mistake.
Sallie may be the greatest recruiter on earth. But that's not a reason – by itself – to promote her into a role where she manages a team of thirteen other recruiters. If all she ever wanted to do was to do her job well and make a little more money in the process...reward her. Don't force her to lead a team, which she has no interest in and is killing her slowly. *Solution: Promote people in the organization that have the technical knowledge AND have shown both the potential and interest in leading.*

#82:
If you want to truly master your time, invest 10% of your time planning how you will use the other 90%.

#83:

Don't allow butt-awful leaders to lead teams.
Some managers in leadership roles are mean, surly, rude, offensive, and specialize in striking fear into the hearts of the team members. That's great if you're Darth Vader or some super-villain in a comic book – but not if you're a paid professional leader. The days of crime bosses are over. Leaders must use influence, clear expectations and inspiration to get results and hold people accountable. Doing this sends the mixed message that: "It's okay for managers to treat you like scum, but we still value you." Yeah, right.

#84:
Getting promoted in HR takes ABILITY and VISIBILITY. Flying under the radar may be GREAT FOR GEESE, but it's a terrible strategy if you want to advance your HR career.

#85:
When complaining about too many priorities, being overworked and your time management problems, remind yourself that you have the EXACT number of hours in a day as Bill Gates, Madonna, Steve Jobs, Oprah Winfrey...and your HR role model.

#86:
If you're an HR leader, let your direct reports hear you say complimentary things about them to the higher ups.

#87:
One year after you leave college, if you're knocking it out of the park, no one will care what your GPA was.

#88:
Look for trusted confidants to bond with, reward and take with you as you climb the ladder in HR. As you move your career forward, they will grow too and will help support your continued success.

#89:
Mentor those who are of a different race, gender, sexual preference, or disability than you are. You will grow as much from the experience as your mentees will from your advice.

#90:
PRE-WIRE YOUR PITCH.
Before giving a formal presentation to sell any new HR program or idea, *get input* from and *pre-sell* the major decision-makers -- long BEFORE they walk through the meeting room door to hear your final pitch.

#91 - #110:
Twenty BIG goals to tackle that will easily place you among the top 5% of all HR professionals:

1. Getting 20 recommendations on LinkedIn.
2. Publishing an article once a year on your specialty.
3. Developing a free white paper on your specialty downloaded by 500 HR people.
4. Writing an HR book.
5. Speaking at local or national SHRM conference.
6. Conducting a webinar, workshop, talk or speech on your specialty.
7. Starting your own HR blog.
8. Starting a group on LinkedIn.
9. Giving a lecture or teaching an HR class at a local university.
10. Creating a brown-bag lecture series.
11. Become an officer in a network or trade association.
12. Getting a twitter account and attracting 500 meaningful followers.
13. Developing a software program on your specialty.
14. Running your HR department as a profit center.
15. Attaining HR certification.
16. Clearly defining how you are different than every other HR professional.
17. Making yourself available as an expert for news stories.
18. Producing a YouTube video on your specialty.
19. Coaching and running Train-the-trainers on your specialty.
20. Editing or contributing to your organization's e-zine or newsletter.

#111:
The cruel power of JUST ONE.

The worst number in managing your HR career is JUST ONE. Just ONE of anything.

Just ONE higher up who thinks you're great.

Just ONE direct report who is indispensible.

Just ONE mentor providing you with advice.

Just ONE resume you're using for your job search.

Just ONE source of income for your livelihood.

Avoid having JUST ONE. They are limiting and unforgiving. Replace them instead with backups, contingencies and plan B's.

#112:

David Ogilvy, the well-known advertising wizard who founded the Ogilvy & Mather advertising agency, never spent a day in HR, but had an orientation practice that all HR leaders would appreciate. He established a wonderful tradition of welcoming new leaders in his organization with a gift of five wooden dolls, each smaller than the other, one inside the other. When the recipient finally gets to the fifth little doll, the smallest doll, and opens it, he finds this message:

"If each of us hires people who are smaller than we are, we shall become a company of dwarfs, but if each of us hires people who are bigger than we are, we shall become a company of giants."

#113:
Dress for the job you want, not the job you have.
If a busy executive is put off by your wrapping, they're not likely to dig deeper to discover your gifts - no matter how many of them make up your package.

#114:
When traveling on the business, put a card in your wallet with your name, your phone number, the phone number of a friend/relative and the HOTEL YOU'RE STAYING AT --- just in case.

#115:

To influence, persuade and really connect with people at a deep and emotional level, speak to them in their language -- using THEIR WORDS, not yours.

#116:
Walk the plant floor.

If you're in HR at a manufacturing location, it is utter lunacy to think that staying in your office and doing email is work. Talk to your employees, managers and suppliers on the shop floor to get a pulse beat on your organization. Regularly. If you don't have to buy a new pair of shoes every six months, you're not doing your job.

#117:

Refuse to lead any major company-wide training program your executives won't attend -- because it will FAIL. In many companies, HR leaders say: "Yes, we conduct (diversity and inclusion) training for everyone, but our Vice Presidents haven't attended." Don't let them off the hook. In fact, take them and your CEO through the training FIRST. Execs cannot reinforce any training they've not experienced themselves. And besides, when the rest of the organization sees that the senior team has taken and are committed to the training, then they'll fall in line too.

#118:
When given the choice, think BIG.

It takes almost the same of amount of time and energy to work on TINY projects in human resources as it takes to manage MASSIVE ones. But the massive ones are the ones which give you massive rewards.

#119:
As an HR leader, you must know when to quarterback and when to cheerlead. Quarterback and call the plays when you can make a big difference. Stay on the sidelines and cheerlead your team on when they can make a bigger impact than you can. Don't quarterback when you should be cheerleading. And, don't cheerlead when you should be quarterbacking.

#120 - #131:
A dozen ways to make people FEEL SPECIAL -- without MONEY.

1. Praise them privately and publicly for their contributions.
2. Appoint them to stand in for you at important meetings.
3. Provide them with opportunities to interact with senior management.
4. Invite them to collaborate with you on important projects.
5. Bring them with you to meetings with higher-ups.
6. Ask for their advice on key issues and problems.
7. Put them on teams & committees for exposure and learning.
8. Mention them in company and industry publications.
9. Get them a senior executive as a mentor.
10. Assign them as advisors or mentors to others.
11. Ask the CEO to drop by their office.
12. Feature them on your organization's web page.

#132:

Look for something positive in every colleague you deal with and focus on that attribute intently when dealing with them...especially your HATERS.

#133:
If you are questioned as part of a workplace investigation, if you tell the truth the situation becomes part of your past. If you lie, it becomes part of your future.

#134:
In political power struggles involving higher ups, don't pick sides if you don't know for certain who's going to be in charge.

#135:
Your job in Human Resources won't take care of you when you are sick. Your friends, spouse, partner, relatives and parents will. Stay in touch.

#136:
You will never, ever regret any money you've spent on flowers, thank you cards or books...with ONE exception (see #137).

#137:
Visit your colleagues when they are in the hospital or at funerals for their loved ones. You only need to stay a few minutes. Sending them gifts or flowers DOES NOT SUBSTITUTE FOR YOUR PRESENCE.

#138:
When an employee is upset, they generally want understanding and empathy BEFORE they want your advice.

#139:
Have your own geek squad...by becoming friends with a couple of IT experts. Once a year, consult them on how you can eliminate paper, procedures or anything else that slows down your personal productivity. Properly using and applying the best technology will give you a competitive edge over your peers, while failure to upgrade will quickly put you behind and unable to compete effectively.

#140:

Any organization-wide survey led by HR will raise people's expectations for change. So don't ask any questions on the survey that you don't plan to take action on, otherwise you will make things worse. Yes, this includes questions about compensation. And yes, no one is ever happy with their pay no matter how competitively well-benchmarked your pay practices are. If you can't change it, don't ask about it.

#141:

The real purpose of a PowerPoint presentation is to get people to *listen*, not look. It can be tempting to pack your slides with extra information to look smart or give your audience extra value. But the most effective power point slides are clear, concise and terse. Limit text to a few phrases, subtitles, or talking points – five or six is usually the maximum. Less is more. *Save your best material for the words you speak.*

#142:

Stress in HR has many causes: unpopular HR programs, dissatisfied employees, unsupportive senior leaders, aggressive deadlines on projects, tight budgets during business downturns, demanding clients and the expectations of your boss. Studies show that performance increases with stress but only up to a point. When anxiety due to stress is too high, performance decreases and exhaustion is reached much more quickly.

#143:
A great HR leader makes imperfect decisions.

It is rare for you to have enough time to collect all the data to support a big decision. You've got to weigh the time, effort and expense to do it against the potential benefits...as well as the danger of delaying the decision. The great HR leader knows:

- When to make a good, workable decision (most of the time) and when to attempt to make the perfect decision.
- When to live with and when to correct a bad decision previously made.
- That no decision or a late decision is almost always worse than a bad decision.
- That sometimes a poor decision is made right in follow-up.
- That even the best decision-makers make mistakes, and that a leader is properly judged on their long-term track record of success.

#144:

Overtly or covertly competing against your peers will increase their resentment towards you. Compete against yourself instead and let others judge whether you are better than your peers.

#145:

The fastest way to increase your network of admirers and supporters is to regularly acknowledge their help publicly.

#146:

Humility and modesty are signs of great character that you should demonstrate regularly. However, the two times you should not be modest are during your ANNUAL PERFORMANCE REVIEW and on your RESUME.

#147:

Never assume that you can keep any merger, downsizing, or major organization change a secret in your company. You can't. And, the longer it takes you to make an announcement, the more people will find out - even if you use confidentiality agreements. Count on it. SO WORK QUICKLY. And, if confronted, just avoid commenting rather than DENY or LIE about the truth. If you mislead, your credibility will suffer and trust between you and your people will be jeopardized. Forever.

#148:
In building your leadership and HR competencies, do not be afraid of going slowly and deliberately. Only be afraid of STANDING STILL.

#149:
To measure how effective you are as an HR leader, count up the number of people who follow you when they really don't have to.

#150:

Don't ever dismantle ANY successful HR program or process until you know why it was established in the first place. All change isn't necessarily a good thing.

#151:

Jack Welch as CEO of GE spent 70% of his time on people development. If it's good enough for him, it's good enough for you.

#152-163:
12 amazingly simple ways to double your personal productivity

- Have a list of people to whom you can immediately rely on to execute tasks, problems and ideas...then delegate MORE to them to leverage their talents, skills, contacts and resources.

- **Learn and maximize use of the latest technology, computers, software to increase your speed & efficiency.**

- Seek out and ask the best people in your HR specialty for their advice and insights.

- **Raise expectations and ask more from your staff after you've provided them with better training, coaching and treatment.**

- Get more from yourself by increasing your knowledge, skill, stamina, and energy. On the latter, hit the gym more often.

- **Get the information you need faster by being CRYSTAL CLEAR on what you want and WHEN you want it. Don't delay, be put off or accept no for an answer.**

- Cut your appointment block time in half – replace 30 minute meetings with 15 minute ones.

- **Create online systems that can "automatically" provide your clients with new HR policies, your insights, advice, best practices or coaching...in your absence or while you work on other projects.**

- Adapt ideas or best practices from outside of your department, your company or HR.

- **Break or reinvent the rules so things get done faster.**

- Say no to trivial requests and be conservative in what you commit your time to – but keep your word.

- **Drive for maximum success in every action you take.**

#164:

If you've got talent, people will want more of your time. Saying no to loud people gives you the space and resources to say yes to important opportunities where you can have tremendous impact.

#165:

Game-changing new HR ideas are succinct, yet descriptive. If you can't boil your HR idea down far enough so you can describe it in a few words on the back of a business card, it's far too complex to be understood. To cut through people's mental clutter, it's got to be a something you, your team and your clients can "get" in seconds. *Example: "30-Minute Performance Appraisals."* If brands like Wheaties ("Breakfast of Champions") or White Castle ("Food You Crave") can describe their billion-dollar products concisely and memorably, you can do the same thing with your HR idea or program.

#166:

Every HR professional will have a special moment when he or she is tapped on the shoulder to do a very special thing unique to them. It is a tragedy if that person is you and that moment finds you unprepared for the work that could become your finest hour.

#167:

Never take a problem to your boss without a few solutions - even if your solutions aren't perfect. **You're getting paid to think, not whine.**

#168:

Google Yourself.

If you're interviewing for an HR job, don't think that the person you're interviewing with for one hour isn't going to take quick five seconds to GOOGLE YOU. So, check yourself first.

If you don't have a web site, if you've never given a speech to an organization, if you've never written any articles for HR trade publications, if you've never done any significant work in community or charity programs, then nothing will show up about you online. And, that's a problem.

On the hand, I've just given you a formula for HR success: make your own web site, speak at an HR workshop, write articles, and involve yourself in the community.

Make the person you're interviewing with excited about meeting with you.

#169:

When you look back on all you've done in HR, you will get much more satisfaction from the pleasure you've brought to other people lives, rather than the times you outdid or defeated them.

#170:
It pays to be authentic.

Some years ago, I was at lunch in Chicago in a fancy restaurant, with some Pepsi HR executives from our New York corporate office. When the salads came, there were too many forks on the table to choose from, and I wasn't quick enough to watch which one everyone else picked up. I was honestly confused. So I asked the guy next to me which fork to start with. About six months later, this guy transferred to Chicago and became my boss. He told me that, at that moment at lunch, even though he'd never met me before his trust in me skyrocketed, simply because I was willing to admit I didn't know which fork to use. (I've since learned the "from-the-outside-in" rule)

#171:
If possible, don't decline a key operational assignment outside of HR, or an HR role close to the seat of power at your corporate headquarters or an international HR assignment in India or China. The experience you'll get is indispensible & will exponentially enlarge your career options.

#172:
Take long weekends and exhaust all your vacation time. In most organizations, you either use it or lose it. And losing it isn't worth it.

#173:
Invest 10% of your income every year to your own training and development. If you work for a company, ask them to subsidize or pay for your training fully. If your company is not interested in your professional development, LEAVE.

#174:
Get a good spiral-bound notebook or a mobile electronic device and take it with you everywhere to take meeting notes, jot down phone-mail messages or capture your ideas. Using this as your on-going business journal allows you to keep all your communications in one place.

#175:
Embrace the 10-minute Wallow Rule.
When you are working on a task and something occurs unexpectedly that, at the time, seems like an unfortunate event – if you have to, give yourself ten minutes just to wallow in your pain. You can feel sorry for yourself …scream, curse, cry, complain bitterly or do whatever you need to do. However, when the ten minutes are up, you got to quit whining and immediately go back to being proactive your life.

#176:
Leave your office building for a few minutes at least once every day, even if it's January and it's below zero outside. It will clear your head and provide you with a fresh perspective.

#177:

Commuting long distances to work isn't a bad thing, you just need a good reason for doing it -- such as loving your job or loving your house. **The longer the commute, the better your reason needs to be.**

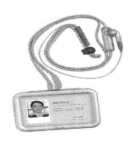

#178:

Become buddies with the guard in the lobby because someday you'll forget your ID badge.

#179:

If your HR job is repetitive or can be documented in a manual, someone else can do it cheaper or it can be outsourced. You need to figure out what makes you special in this role or you're expendable.

#180:

Have lunch once a month with someone outside the company who someday might hire you.

#181:
How to read your client's mind.

Recently, I was summoned to the office of the CEO of a large and fast-growing private company. I was being considered for a very important, very big, very lucrative HR consulting assignment that I wanted badly. In the 45 minutes or so of this meeting, we actually dealt with the matter at hand for only 10 minutes, and I listened for half of those minutes. For the other 35 minutes, I mostly listened to the CEO talk about his problems of the day, expound on his business philosophy, brag about his most recent big deal, and unintentionally tell me EXACTLY what he wanted to hear from me to make our deal. So, I sat there and quietly "read his mind." Try it.

#182:
Your personal market value declines every single day you stay with a company or an HR department going downhill. Don't be the last one to leave.

#183:
Reorganizations mean someone will lose his or her job. To protect yourself, get on the task force that will make the recommendations.

#184 – #186:
Three brutal, proven truths about implementing organization change.

Truth #1: It's generally easier to kill a department or organization, than to change it substantially.

Truth #2: If you need to dramatically change your organization FAST, create a crisis. When people are under the gun, they will face reality more directly, be less selfish and band together to address the common enemy. If you already have a crisis, use it to upgrade the organization, make it more productive and make needed organization changes. *A crisis is a terrible thing to waste.*

Truth #3: If you can't create a crisis, create a pilot. Introduce change to a small group within the company with those already favorably disposed towards embracing it:
- Work out the bugs with this prototype group.
- Protect them from the rest of the organization.
- Involve your best and most progressive people.
- Reward and recognize them for taking risks.
- Once it's successful, hold this up to the rest of the organization as the model they should emulate.

#187:
If you want a highly successful experience, don't volunteer to be a meeting facilitator without having some knowledge of the content or subject matter being discussed. Pure meeting facilitation skills are NOT enough to guide the group to a successful conclusion.

#188:
Saying no to your clients by telling them: *"It's HR policy"* simply angers them. That's the corporate equivalent of your parents saying: *"Because I said so."*

#189:
Avoid getting stale. **For a jolt of HR inspiration, a fresh perspective or new ideas:** go visit your one of your most progressive manufacturing sites, attend a SHRM conference or high tech trade show...or schedule a benchmarking trip to a leading company outside of your industry.

#190:
YOU WILL NEVER BE ABLE TO ATTAIN ULTIMATE HR SUCCESS AT A COMPANY YOU WOULD BE PUBLICLY ASHAMED TO SHOW YOUR LOYALTY TO OR WHOSE PRODUCTS AND SERVICES YOU WOULDN'T HAVE IN YOUR HOME OR RECOMMEND TO YOUR FAMILY.

#191- #205:

15 COUNTER-OFFERS
You Can Make To Retain
Your Best People
...WITHOUT GIVING THEM MORE MONEY

1. Change their manager
2. Give them a chance to lead a team
3. Provide them more exposure to senior leadership
4. Change their job to include new responsibilities
5. Offer them a rotation to a different job
6. Give them new, exciting clients to work with
7. Transfer them to a new location
8. Assign them to a new, innovative work team
9. Offer them work on a breakthrough new project
10. Provide them access to new technology or tools
11. Assign them employees to mentor or train
12. Set new challenging, inspirational stretch goals
13. Provide more training, an opportunity to learn and stay on the leading edge
14. Let them work remotely or from home -- fully or partially.
15. Or offer them ALL OF THE ABOVE!

#206 - #215:
⭐10 WAYS TO WOW YOUR CEO

1. **Know the top 3 business problems that keep your CEO up at night** – Check out their speeches, memos and write-ups. Pay particular attention to communications they send to all employees on the company intranet. Read their meeting agendas. Ask their direct reports or their admin, or just ask them what their priorities are. Show them that you absolutely share their passion for the business and its challenges.

2. **Know their top 3 priorities for HR** - Make sure you know specifically what their priorities and expectations are from you and the HR function. Don't guess, ask them. At least one item on their list will surprise you. Probe deeper and ask them to quantify their metrics of success for HR, if they can. Business conditions change often, so make sure you confirm these expectations quarterly. If it is tough arranging a meeting with them, drop them an e-mail noting what you believe their priorities are and ask them to comment on it.

3. **Know what information they really value** - CEO's are swamped with information…but one thing they're keen on is knowing their competition. If you know how their direct competitor "does things" in a key area of interest to them, you'll become an instant hero. Talk to consultants, suppliers and former employees that now work as competitors.

4. **Don't be boring.** Be interesting, impressive and exciting as an individual. Jack up your energy level and enthusiasm when you meet with them. Be direct and add pop to your language…but be yourself.

5. **Know the top 3 future problems they will soon be facing** - Track issues facing the industry, read articles by the top performers in your industry and reports written by industry analysts. Be able to discuss these at any time.

6. **Show them how HR makes or saves the organization money.** In your conversations about your HR initiatives emphasize dollars, numbers and results...not words and process. Words like competitive advantage, ROI, revenue, or cost savings will especially grab their attention.

7. **Find out what it takes (what others have done) to become one of their trusted advisors** – Track the success and failure that others have had in gaining their confidence so that they will turn to you when they need some "honest" advice. Identify people that they currently "seek out" for advice. Ask them what they did to gain the CEO's confidence. Also ask their admin.

8. **Give the CEO "heads-up" warnings** -- CEO's hate to be surprised. Become known one of the people who can help cover their butt by giving them early alerts about things about to happen and they will learn to respect you. Identify people that seem to be "the first to know" and put together an early warning network and use it to build your reputation as an "anticipator."

9. **Be quick on your feet, agile and flexible.** Be prepared to provide them with multiple options on big issues and have more than one answer in your hip pocket for their questions. However, don't be shy in telling them what ONE thing they should do. Have a strong point of view.

10. **Be proactive and aim to overdeliver**, not just satisfy them. Be optimistic and don't "whine". Forget the words "No" and "I can't" and replace them with the phrases "right away" and "We'll find a way" to get things done.

#216:
C players don't hire A players. So don't hire C players.

#217:

Get any verbal commitments about future promotions or career moves IN WRITING before you accept your new HR job. Undocumented promises of future potential are almost always overstated and are often not honored – sometimes even if you DO have a signed agreement. Protect your interests.

#218:

If you're the HR pro in charge, do all you can to resist across-the-board layoffs. In a business downturn, consider first:

- Freezing new hiring
- Eliminating temporary workers
- Using voluntary leaves
- Reducing the pay of the most senior executives
- Eliminating redundant or unnecessary work
- Encouraging early retirements
- But if you must layoff, use it as an opportunity to eliminate poor performers and marginal players.

#219:
Never hire one of the big HR consulting firms without doing a little haggling on price.

#220:
If you want your audience's full attention, give handout materials AFTER your presentation, never before.

#221:
Never let the odds, naysayers and corporate politics keep you from standing up for what you know in your heart to be just and right.

#222:
WHEN YOUR BOSS INTRODUCES YOU TO THEIR SPOUSE OR PARTNER, SAY: "I HAVE LOOKED FORWARD TO MEETING YOU, BECAUSE THE BOSS BRAGS ABOUT YOU ALL THE TIME."

#223:
Ask yourself if what you're doing today is getting you closer to where you want to be tomorrow.

#224:

Live the boomerang principle.

Give away that which you most want to receive back.
If you want help, help others.
If you want trust, trust others.
If you want admiration, give it away.

If you want great colleagues at work, be one.
If you want a great team, be a great team member.
IT'S LIKE THROWING A BOOMERANG – WHAT YOU TOSS OUT, COMES BACK TO YOU. **That's how it works.**

#225:

Great HR leaders are servants. They help their people do well, look good and allow them to receive the recognition. Poor HR leaders lord over their people, take over often and then blame them for mistakes.

#226:

If you work in employee benefits, keep in mind that programs that pay employees to work and stay healthy are much less costly than programs that pay for them when they're out and sick.

#227:

AVOID BUILDING HUGE EMPIRES.

IN A LEAN ORGANIZATION THAT IS SOMEWHAT SHORTHANDED, PEOPLE HAVE LESS TIME TO PLAY OFFICE POLITICS, PROCRASTINATE ON PRIORITIES OR WASTE TIME. MOST HIGH PERFORMERS FIND IT MORE FUN TO BE OVERWORKED THAN TO BE UNDERWORKED.

#228:
How To Attract The Best Talent
To Your Department

- **Build and position your department as the "talent launching pad"** for your organization or industry...the place where new people can develop their careers fast and "must" pass through on their way to the top.

- **Clarify the future.** Everyone wants to know where he or she will be in a few years. Give people a projection of where they might reasonably expect to be in 2-3 years if things go well...or how valuable they'll be to another organization, if things don't.

- **Hire globally.** Position your department as the place where diverse talent from around the world are recognized, rewarded and promoted. Give specific examples of successful people who have passed through your department and how they've progressed their careers.

- **Have the best, state-of-the-art talent development systems in place.** Ensure everyone has a fabulous career development plan for maxing out their skills and potential.

- **Give them a "wow" factor to brag about to their family and friends.** This could include high profile projects, high tech toys, a great location, an awesome work area or mentoring by a superstar executive.

- **Surround your people with great colleagues.** "A" players want to be around other people that help make them better.

- **Be a "talent exporter," not a selfish hoarder.** Keep the best people only as long as they are growing and developing. Then voluntarily "give them up" to other departments where they can continue their upward trajectory.

#229:
How to GIVE an awesome 30 minute speech

1. Speak for 22 minutes straight from the heart.
2. No slides.
3. No handouts.
4. No flip charts.
5. And if you must open with a joke, let it be on you.

#230:
How to PREPARE to give an awesome 30 minute speech

1. Write it all out.
2. Put in five hours rehearsing your speech aloud beforehand.
3. If there's Q&A, anticipate every question and answer.
4. Be prepared for at least one question you didn't anticipate. Your answer to that question will emerge from everything you prepared beforehand.

#231:

Half of every HR document or power point presentation is typically very clear. The problem is the OTHER HALF...cut out that piece of the document and its impact will improve.

#232:

If you're restructuring your HR department, you'll find that the best structure on earth will be organized around your key clients ...and will be filled with HR pros who multi-functional, multi-skilled with excellent people skills who are passionate about satisfying their clients' needs.

#233:
Anyone that has become off-the-charts successful in HR does so by getting brilliant on their business. Not the HR business, but the business that's providing you with a paycheck. So, stop asking for a seat at the table - sit down - give an opinion - or leave the room.

#234 - #245:
A dozen things every HR person should know about their business

1. The company's current share price (if it is publicly traded)
2. Profit (bottom line) over the last two years
3. Revenue growth (top line) over the last two years
4. Key productivity (cost management) strategies
5. Primary product brands or services offered
6. How the company makes money
7. How customers are being satisfied
8. How the product is manufactured or service is delivered
9. How products/services are developed, marketed and sold
10. Customer retention and attraction strategies
11. Key suppliers and customers
12. What gives your company a competitive advantage

#246:
At business strategy meetings, you know you've arrived when....

1. The CFO brings quarterly financial updates.
2. The Marketing VP brings the new product roll out strategy.
3. And you bring: (1) software that describes the impact of your HR initiatives on the P&L and, (2) metrics and side-by-side comparisons that show the contribution and engagement of your work-force against that of your biggest competitor.

#247:

Rapid talent development occurs when people are promoted SLIGHTLY before they're ready and are stretched SLIGHTLY out of their comfort zone. However, they also need safety nets so they don't drown completely.

#248:

High performers thrive on big challenges, clear goals and meritocracy. To retain them, keep these in steady supply.

#261- #265:
Five ways to move faster in HR:
- Limit consensus building.
- Have fewer meetings.
- Empower your people and their teams more.
- Provide clear accountability for decisions.
- Have more aggressive deadlines.

#249:

Take the first step to soothe any "ruffled feathers" that may exist if you were brought into your new HR role above someone who thought they should have had your job...especially if this person is now on your team. Don't depend on your boss to do this for you. No matter how well your boss may have done it, it will not substitute for you making a special effort to build this relationship.

#250:
Tell your high potentials that they are high potential. Nothing is gained by hiding this information...other than allowing them to get hired by another company that will tell them that to their face.

#251:
You don't get promoted in HR unless you promote yourself. Just working hard and expecting that your results alone will be recognized, noticed, or will be appreciated guarantees one thing and one thing only: old age. And focusing on doing what you do better than anyone else and trusting that that alone is enough, guarantees you one thing and one thing only: a long life laboring in oblivion.

#252:
If there's nothing WOW or special about your work, you won't get noticed and you won't get paid much either.

#253:
Have someone to confide in that you can share your out-of-the box, half-baked ideas and inklings with who won't laugh.

#254:
You change things by standing up when it's NOT popular.

#255:
You have become a GREAT coach when you can give real, authentic, accurate feedback without pissing people off.

#256:
When coaching someone, try asking them: "What's the biggest opportunity you're letting pass you by right now?" Their answer will speak volumes.

#257:
A coachable moment has arrived when someone says:

- Do you have a minute...?
- There's something I'd like to run by you...
- What would you do in a situation like this...?
- I'm stuck...
- I'd like your advice on...

In these moments you can improve an employee's performance, enhance your business or make a difference in someone's life. Be ready.

#258 - #262:

Five magic questions. The world's simplest and most powerful HR coaching you can do starts by asking these five questions:

- What makes it difficult to get your job done?
- What do you need to get smarter at?
- In what areas are you confused?
- What excites you most about working here?
- What frustrates most you about working here?

You can build an entire HR career successfully by doing nothing more than helping frustrated individuals, teams and organizations address the answers to these questions.

#263:

The secret to remaining non-union. Unions focus on lower level needs like security, pay and safety. You concentrate on these things too...PLUS higher level needs like recognition, meaning, fulfillment and building a great place to work...and you'll keep the union out every time.

#264:

Be proactive with your boss. Get to her before she comes to you. Know her priorities and get smarter on the things that drive her success.

#265 - #272:
Eight Ways HR can contribute to
IMPROVED PRODUCTIVITY

- By creating performance management programs that drop poor performing managers and employees quickly.

- **By ensure that mega-rewards are provided to employees who deliver mega-results.**

- By ensuring that at least 50% of a manager's annual raise is based on their success in managing talent and increasing people productivity.

- **By putting reward systems in place for sharing best productivity practices between managers, teams, departments and businesses.**

- By ensuring HR policies support treating employees like mature adults, minimizing rules and ensuring that those who act immaturely are terminated.

- **By prioritizing HR time and services to focus on jobs and the HR programs with the highest impact. All jobs and programs are not created equal.**

- By making sure each HR program focuses on performance improvement - not equality and "sameness" - and significant differentiation based on performance.

- By not neglecting to recognize *effort, past loyalty* and *seniority*...along with rewarding results, major milestones and continuous improvement.

#273:

To gain the same reputation as the Finance people in your organization, simply measure and manage your human resources results with the same rigor and discipline that your Finance department measures and manages the financial results of the firm. If you're not sure, partner with your Finance leader on how to best do this for HR.

#274:

Before you start your first day in a new HR job, check out your new clients, staff members and direct reports on LinkedIn, Facebook or on Google. Since many have already no doubt checked you out, you should return the favor. Use the information to help build rapport or to establish common ground. Knowing who went to your same school, who likes to golf or play tennis, who is reading the latest Ulrich book, or who knows the same people you know is a heck of a lot better than an awkward silence after "I'm doing fine, thank you."

#275:

When you visit a workplace similar to yours, go with the objective of identifying 3 best practices that you can bring back and immediately reapply. If you can't, don't go or don't return.

#276:
You get the best efforts from others not by LIGHTING a fire beneath them, but by BUILDING a fire within.

#277 - #284:
Eight deadly signs that it's time to find a better HR opportunity

1. You're not having fun anymore.
You dread the thought of going to work. You used to get up in the morning anxious to get going. But now each day takes more effort than it used to. If you have to press that snooze button three or four more times than normal, then it's time to dust off the resume.

2. You don't see things improving.
You've tried to change important elements of your job that you feel must change and that are within your control. It could be that you're doing more grunt work than you'd like. It could be that you're working with a client you don't like. If could be that you've tried to take responsibility for making things better. However, if repeated efforts to solve the problem have failed, you face the tough choice: Stay where the conditions will bother you, or find a different environment.

3. You're dead-ended.
There's no way for you to grow, learn or move up. Perhaps you've worked hard, performed well, and now there is no place for you to go. If this is the case, maybe your next step is to go elsewhere. If you stay put, you're likely not going to be growing and developing.

4. You're not on "the list."
Yes, that list. You know the one. The one that all promotion-minded HR folks want to be on. After busting your butt, you've been told you're a solid performer and valuable member of the team, but no one's lobbying for you as a candidate for the next

level. You're excluded from the "highly confidential" meetings that you used to attend at one time. You've been told to "hang in there" and keep working on your weaknesses.

5. Your company results are in the toilet.
The numbers suck and no rebound is in sight. The organization is going through the second wave of downsizing...in the last six months. Top performers are bailing fast, like rats from a sinking ship. Your company needs you, but only to help deliver more upcoming bad news to employees.

6. You've lost your influence.

People, who used to hang on your every word, now aren't listening to you anymore. Or they aren't laughing at your jokes anymore. It could be that the joke's on you. When you look around, you notice that some of your best past supporters and champions are no longer around. If the folks that are now in place seem to roll their eyes and humor you — it could be time to make a move. If you're feeling ineffective, it could be that for some reason you longer have credibility to be the agent of change you must be in HR. This is not good news.

7. You have nothing new to put on your resume.
You don't have any new, game-changing projects on the horizon. No new assignments that you're excited about. You're only there because you love the people you work with and you've built strong bonds with them, both on and off the job.

8. You are physically reacting to being at work.
You suffer from headaches and other stress related symptoms while at work. You are constantly agitated while on the job. You have a short fuse with your family and friends. You seek out confrontation where none exists. Negativity is affecting every area of your life.

#285:

Exceptional success comes from spending more time using your CORE STRENGTHS and less time working on the stuff you suck at.

#286:

Take time to celebrate. Don't take your victories for granted. It's too easy to simply move on to your next goal without acknowledging, appreciating and taking time to truly savor your "wins."

#287:

GIVE BACK. COMMIT TO TAKING A PERCENTAGE OF YOUR EARNINGS OR YOUR TIME AND USE THEM TO MAKE A DIFFERENCE FOR SOMEONE. IF YOU DON'T THINK YOU CAN, THEN STARTING MAKING MORE MONEY OR WORKING MORE EFFICIENTLY.

#288:

Evil, underhanded, devious little ways to find out if employees in your company are looking for another job...

- Search online job boards for resumes of people you know.
- Check to see if their profile on LinkedIn or Facebook has been recently updated.
- Have a recruiter to call them to see how fast they respond.
- Run a blind ad to attract your own employees who may be looking.
- Attend local job fairs to see if any of your employees attend.
- Look at the timing of previous job changes on their resume to see if there is a predictable pattern of when are likely to leave this job (18 months to two years).
- Have your Benefits Department notify you when employees ask questions about liquidating their stock, 401k accounts, leaving a job or retiring.
- Look for an increased attendance at outside career conferences and workshops geared towards increasing their network.
- Watch closely for who has an unexplained recent pattern of absences on Fridays or Mondays.
- Look for a sudden interest in gaining visibility by holding office in local professional associations.

#289:
You should be able to put your HR strategy on a single sheet of paper. If you can't, it's much too complex and you won't be able to quickly energize and align your HR team behind it.

#290:

If you're in HR in a unionized organization, you have an obligation to communicate and build trusting relationships directly with your employees…despite your relationship with your union. Most employees who are union members are decent people trying to raise their kids. They want to work hard, want to be successful, and are generally proud of their company. They also want to know what's going on in the organization…good or bad. And, they need to hear it from DIRECTLY FROM YOU AND THE MANAGEMENT TEAM FIRST, not their union leaders.

#291:

All clients aren't good for you. If you can, get rid of clients from hell or those that don't bring out your professional best. Life is too short. No matter what you've been told, the client is NOT always right.

#292:
To really differentiate yourself from the rest of the HR pack, start a blog.

If you don't already have a blog, go start one right this minute. If you need inspiration, check out HR blogs by: Kris Dunn, Michael Haberman, Lisa Rosendahl, Lance Haum or Angelique Kennedy.

Your blog is your living resume. It shows how you think. It shows how you write. It shows what's important to you. It can draw career or entrepreneurial opportunities to you that you would not believe.

What's your HR passion? Compensation Design. Leadership Development. Labor Negotiations. Resume Writing. Diversity Programs. Educate us on your passion and help all of us grow through your blog. Employers of the future will love bloggers. Microsoft and Apple love 'em now – they're ahead of the curve and they get it. Frankly, other companies haven't caught on – at least, not yet.

Bloggers are mentors and employers love hiring mentors – they raise everybody's performance. One caveat, this does not give you the right to be a raging lunatic on your blog, but is the chance for you to show off what you're capable of doing, what you've done, and what you can do for others who can really benefit from your expertise.

#293:
Whether negotiating the salary for your next job or negotiating a union labor contract....the person who MOST WANTS the negotiation to succeed has the LEAST BARGAINING POWER. No matter how badly you want it, appear neutral or only moderately interested. The more you can make the other party want it worse than you do, the better deal you'll get.

#294:
Remember the "walk away" law.
As painful as it might be, in negotiating you'll never know the other person's final offer until you get up and walk away. Leverage and power is on the side of the person who can walk out without flinching or batting an eye.

#295:
Never consider _any_ negotiation final. If you are not a happy camper with the results of the negotiation, ask to re-open the discussion.

#296:

To accelerate your progress on any project, replace fuzzy expectations with S.M.A.R.T. objectives. These are objectives that are:

- Specific
- Measureable
- Achievable
- Realistic
- Time-Bound

Most people hesitate to move quickly when faced with ambiguous expectations...but will speed up their movement when attracted to and inspired by crystal clear goals.

#297:

BE COURAGEOUS. COURAGE IS DOING WHAT YOU'RE SCARED TO DO. YOUR OPPORTUNITIES IN HR WILL SHRINK OR EXPAND IN DIRECT PROPORTION TO THE COURAGE YOU SHOW.

#298:

Join or establish a mastermind group outside of your organization made up of your professional peer group. You need the diversity of thought so these should be HR and non-HR types. Regularly connect with these people to bounce ideas, test your theories, celebrate successes, and to share your lessons learned. It's a great way to acquire wisdom and extend yours to others.

#299:
If you're a new HR leader, hold a very brief "icebreaking" meeting with your staff on your first day. Being "missing-in-action" on day one is a horrible way to hit the ground running in your new HR leader-ship role. Your new direct reports will be understandably curious and concerned about what the new boss is like, so don't keep them waiting and wondering. Many will have already googled you or looked up your profile on LinkedIn and may already have developed initial impressions without even having met you. So, take charge imme-diately and begin to connect with your team right away. Here's what you'll want to do in this meeting:

- Express your enthusiasm and optimism about your new HR role.
- Share background information about yourself.
- Discuss your overall preferred style of working.
- Share initial and broad expectations you have of your staff.
- Have your staff to introduce themselves.
- Indicate you'll be setting up one-on-ones in the next few days to get to know people better.
- If some members of your team are in remote loca-tions, conference them into the meeting.
- Focus only on intros, icebreaking, and connecting – that's all! There's plenty of time for everything else.

#300:

When you first join a new company, avoid shoving your old company in the face of your new one. Unless you're asked about it, no one wants to constantly hear you say, "Well, at my old company, we did sales incentive plans this way...." or "When I was at GE, we did performance reviews at a different time in the year." People will get sick of this quickly. This not only sounds like your previous company did everything better, but also makes it look like you miss your old HR job and aren't happy with the new one. **Your focus should be forward, not backward.** Talking about the way you did things at your previous company implies that your head or heart is still there. So, be highly selective in bringing it up. After the first few times, you'll find out that nobody cares.

#301:

Resist the urge to prove yourself the first week in any new HR job. Take advantage of your "honeymoon" period to learn about the new organization before making decisions and acting. Learn about the products and services, the people, and the problems. Ask your new colleagues their opinions about the issues and opportunities. The greater the difference between the old and new company, the longer your learning curve will be.

#302:
SIMPLE RULES FOR WINNING PEOPLE OVER TO YOUR IDEAS

1. Begin each conversation in a friendly manner.
2. Look at things from the other person's perspective.
3. Avoid saying "you're wrong."
4. If you're wrong, be sure to admit it immediately.
5. Be understanding of the other person's thoughts and needs.
6. Get the other person to agree enthusiastically.
7. Avoid arguing.
8. Let the other person talk as much as he or she wants.
9. Let the other person feel the ideas are his (hers).
10. Appeal to each person's nobler motives.

#303:

Toss out those old, torn, dog-eared magazines in your lobby. Replace them with new magazines and colorful brochures about your company. There are only three things that should be happening while your visitors are waiting:

1. Getting them better EDUCATED about your company and how they can profit from its products and services.
2. Getting them more SOLD, committed and enthused about what your company does.
3. Getting them MOTIVATED enough to refer someone else to your company as an employee, client, customer, or shareholder.

#304:

Get rid of the fancy paintings and put up pictures of employees and their families in the entrance of your lobby. This is a proven and successful morale boosting tool for small companies. If your organization is large, rotate the employee pictures in and out frequently.

#305:
Hire high school HONOR STUDENTS to do temporary projects in your workplace. If a kid has the discipline to get good grades, then he or she usually will be a quick study and a more than competent employee. Doing this makes your company's goodwill spread and you will have created a great source for talent. *Tip:* To ensure your success, remember to work with their parents...and interview them as well as the student.

#306:

Don't clutter your schedule with so many trivial and unimportant things that you have no time to accept the spectacular opportunity when it comes along ~ and it will come along.

#307:

Go small to grow BIG. Pick one thing in HR and turn yourself into a "brand" for that one thing. Become so good at it that people seek you out and want to use you as their expert. Become the "go to" person for this HR specialty. (see #2).

#308:

When complimented, watch the size of your head.
Talent is God given. Be humble.
Fame is man-given. Be grateful.
Conceit is self-given. Be careful.
    --Coach John Wooden

#309 - #322:
14 Ways To Turn Your Clients Into Your Biggest Fans

1. **Learn what frustrations and business issues they are struggling with and help them find solutions.** Ask and listen to what your client says. Do this instead of foisting your assumptions, style, knowledge or advice on them.

2. **Become a person they want to partner with.** Carry yourself with self-respect and dignity and professionalism. Yet, be authentic and humble with foibles just like them... someone they enjoy as a person and as an HR pro.

3. **Deliver what you say you will deliver consistently.** Be and keep your word. This builds credibility for you as an HR professional and for your team. Amaze them by delivering on time even when you know in advance you'll be out of the office.

4. **Don't take no for an answer when you know you're right or when you sense your HR client is hesitant, lacks information or is unclear.** Clients value HR professionals who are confident and decisive. Sometimes you'll frustrate the hell out of

your clients, but they will always respect you if you give good counsel, make your arguments fact-based, and keep the organization's best interest at heart.

5. **Help them think for today and tomorrow.** Example: Get them thinking strategically about the talent challenges they could face within their team and how to best handle them. This could include long-term replacements for key people, closing skill gaps within the team, or restructuring their team for more impact. It could also include discussions of the people implications resulting from a sudden decline in the business, merger with a competitor or expansion in the team's role.

6. **Become their trusted advisor.** Become the person that your client can say anything to and let their hair down with – at ANYTIME. Assuming the role of that safe and trusted confidant is one of the most valuable roles you can play with your client. At the end of the day, your ultimate success as an HR pro depends on your ability to build committed trustworthy relationships with them.

7. **Identify ways your client can enhance their effectiveness and success.** Every HR client has underutilized strengths. Help your client discover and leverage theirs. This can be the great way to make the difference and add value. Example: If your client is a great communicator, you might spend time coaching

them on different ways he or she could communicate the role and value of their department in the organization.

8. **When possible, provide your HR clients 2 to 3 options or solutions when they present problems to you.** Then work with them to select and customize the best one(s) to their situation. Example: When talking with a Sales Director about retention strategies for one his top salespeople who may be looking to leave the company, you might suggest enlarging her current territory, a base salary adjustment or a transfer to a more attractive sales region...or some combination. Clients like having choices without feeling that they are backed into a corner.

9. **Insist that your clients provide you with regular feedback on how you're doing in delivering against their needs....then make adjustments based on that feedback.** Regularly ask them what they'd like to see you "stop-start-and-continue." From this very simple question, you'll get answers back like: "I'd like faster turnaround time on compensation decisions" or "We need to move faster on developing the leadership development program we discussed!" Let your clients know that you've heard them and share what changes or actions you'll be taking based on their feedback.

10. **Develop helpful tools that your clients can use without you being there.** Put together one page tip sheets on common issues like interviewing, rewarding performance, leadership, calibrating per-

formance ratings or giving feedback. Have these ready to use as discussion or coaching tools for your clients. You might also refer them to routine or continually changing HR policies and practices on the internet or your company's intranet so that your clients can access the information they need independently. This frees you up to pick up new skills or deliver more value.

11. **Help clients improve their team's effectiveness.** Use team assessments or surveys to help them clarify and enhance their team's development or performance.

12. **Partner with your client on a major change they're looking to implement.** To improve the success of this change, work with them on the communications and people management aspects of this change.

13. **Offer to facilitate a strategic planning retreat with your client to help them identify opportunities take their business or department's effectiveness to the next level.** Challenge your client to set their sights on becoming the very best in their field or area. Aspiration works. Educate clients on themselves. Develop/use individual assessments or surveys to help them discover and leverage their styles, preferences or competencies. Then work with them to identify the talent or HR implications of their new strategy.

14. **Give this list to your clients.** And then ask them to pick 2-3 things they'd like you to concentrate most on this year with them.

#323:

REAL BREAKTHROUGHS and new ideas in HR often show up innocently as interruptions, contradictions, and embarrassing moments provided by total strangers who tell you something you've never heard before or that makes you uncomfortable. Consider these people messengers from the future who are directing you down a new, different or better path.

#324:

An HR person who has done something is almost always far more expert on it than outside consultants who have not. Any HR program that is designed using ONLY consultants, with no contribution from those with personal experience, is absolutely DOOMED to failure.

#325:

The easiest way to end an argument with a colleague is to be the first to say: "I'm sorry." As soon as you say it, the other side will look at you to see if you're sincere. If you are, the tension will begin to evaporate..

#326:
To deal with a detractor, ask them for their advice. Few people can resist being asked for their input. When doing this, you position yourself as open minded and the detractor will often open up to you.

#327:
Everyone is going through something. You're not the only person suffering from money worries, health issues, career dilemmas or relationship problems. That colleague who rudely ignored you when you passed by them in the corridor may have just found out that their spouse lost their job or is worrying about their sick child. Just as you have bad days, so do others. Just as you want them to understand you life, you need to understand theirs.

#328:
Great HR helps creates ORGANIZATIONS THAT WIN and INSPIRING WORKPLACES for employees. If asked, be able to clearly articulate how the HR that you do aligns with these two ideals.

#329:
Bring your REAL self to work. Putting on an act on the job by trying to behave, speak, or act the way you *think* others want you to, is exhausting and uses up valuable mental and emotional energy that doesn't allow you to perform at your best. *Being who you really are gives you confidence.* When you're comfortable with who you are, you exude a confidence that is attractive to your clients and your colleagues. People want to listen to those that are confident and self-assured; they want to hear their advice, they trust their judgement and they'll buy their ideas - sometimes, even if the ideas are BAD.

#330:

Avoid telling your HR staff HOW to do things. Tell them instead WHAT you want to achieve and let them surprise you with their ingenuity.

#331:

Whenever you think you need to REPLACE SOMEONE or ADD TO STAFF, ask yourself these questions first:

- Can we do this job differently?
- Can we outsource it or eliminate it all altogether?
- Why are we even doing this job?
- Can we split the job up among several of the people already on staff?
- Can we use technology to do the job? (For instance, voice mail and direct dial numbers have replaced many receptionist positions.)

#332:

Stay in touch with the great employees who leave you. Often they find the pastures are not truly any greener elsewhere. In fact, once they get there, they may find themselves wishing they'd never left you. After they've been in their new job a couple of weeks, call and see if they would like to come back. If you publish a company newsletter, keep your good former employees on the e-mailing list. **You should also create a LinkedIn group for your company and encourage alumni to participate.** Send them birthday cards inviting them to come back. Even if they don't come back, they can be a tremendous source of referrals.

#333:
Don't offer people a job. Offer them the excitement of joining a cause.

The best recruiters don't sell job candidates on being with the largest company with the most sales, highest profits, top salaries or best benefits...because they often they don't have these things to work with. Instead, they sell the candidate on the PRIDE and FEELING they'll get when they join their organization – and specifically on the OPPORTUNITY to...

- Have an impact on society
- Make a difference in the world
- Be with a company they'll be proud of
- Get respect and be among people they like
- Be recognized and appreciated for their contributions
- Join a team working to achieve a goal they could never reach on their own
- Advance their career FASTER in a brand new organization

If you don't have exceptional pay & benefits to offer, sell the opportunity be a part of something GREAT.

#334:

Great managers count more than you realize.
Research consistently shows that the number one thing
a company can do to retain exceptional people, whether
they are mechanics or vice presidents, is to put them
under an awesome manager. *People don't voluntarily
leave good organizations, they leave poor managers.*
A great manager is typically an "encourager," dedicated
to bringing out the most in their people and has an un-
relenting commitment to retain their best talent.

#335:
*Special project assignments are
fine, but give everyone on your HR
team a client to satisfy. It puts
more of their skin in the game.*

#336:
When communicating a new change
or new HR program ~ if you want it
understood, keep it simple by finding
its ONE core message – its one critical sound bite ~ and then repeat that
over and over again. Simplicity &
repetition works.

#337:

"Improving Business Results Through People."

These are the five simplest words you'll ever hear to describe what HR is all about. You'll never find a more concise and accurate definition of HR than this one. No matter department you work in – compensation, learning and development, labor relations, talent acquisition -- this is what it is all about. Don't complicate it.

#338:

Many struggle with whether to become a generalist or specialist in HR. If you take too long to decide what to do with your HR career, you will find that the decision has already been made for you.

#339:

When introducing and communicating a major HR change beware of long silences. They are often masquerading as resistance with different clothes on.

#340:

The first thing to plan before you begin any labor negotiation is what to do when the other side says "NO." Know your alternatives, backups and Plan B's in advance. When the union presents a curveball you didn't expect:

- Probe to understand why the issue is important to them.
- Listen to alternatives to see if it can be resolved right away.
- If it can't be resolved, then table it.
- If can't be tabled, then call a break and caucus with your negotiating team.

#341:
Your personal packaging matters.
Dress for success. You generally get treated with greater courtesy and respect by senior leaders, colleagues, personal assistants, external consultants (and for that matter merchants, store clerks, waiters and waitresses, airline employees and hotel clerks too!)…when you're dressed for business, rather than when you're in casual clothes.

#342:
It's a good idea to learn from other people's experience but with one caveat: seek out and learn from those with experience who are at the TOP OF THEIR GAME. Falling under the influence of someone headed nowhere will generally lead you to the same destination.

#343:
ONE of the fastest ways to elevate your HR career is to write a book about what you already know about your HR specialty. Your book does not need to be one you sell for money. It's MORE POWERFUL as a tool you can *give away* as your "business card" to prospective clients, employers, or hiring managers. It credentializes your expertise and tells them that you know what you're talking about …even if you really don't.

#344:

Pick a mission or cause outside of the HR field that you deeply believe in. Volunteer your time to support at least one organization committed to this mission. Donate a percentage of your income to it as well. Do it because it's the right thing to do with no expectation of ever getting any pay-back...and remarkably, you'll QUICKLY find new, unexpected opportunities knocking at your door.

#345:

In your role in HR as a coach, do not interact with anyone unless you can make them better and improve their life and career. There's a difference between giving advice based on your experience and giving opinions based on your speculation. You will gain more respect by referring those needing help to someone who truly can.

#346:

It's ok to be a PACK RAT. Keep all your HR stuff. Unfortunately, many of the hot, "new" HR initiatives of the moment are merely recycled versions of those done years earlier. *Examples:* new employee orientation programs or leadership training. When programs like these resurface, your personal archives will give you a leg up – or tell you what not to do.

#347:

Set aside "ONE career hour" a week. If

you're busy doing your job, it's easy to forget to spend some time managing your career. You might spend that hour...

- Revising your resume to make sure it's up-to-date
- Enhancing your LinkedIn profile or requesting more endorsements to support that profile.
- Giving a presentation on your HR specialty at a lunch-and-learn training session to build your skills.
- Networking over coffee or dinner with someone who may someday offer or refer you to your next job.
- Returning all those headhunter calls you've gotten to provide them with a referral -- to keep that relationship going.

If you don't make time to do things like this, it WILL cost you in the long run.

#348:

Too much flexibility in your HR job search DOES NOT work. On your

resume or in job interviews, being open to all job human resources possibilities screams that you're clueless about the kind of job you want. Good recruiters recognize those on "fishing expeditions" in a heartbeat. Pinpoint and communicate confidently the job you want and make sure it's laid out in the HEADLINE on your resume.

#349:
You can't build personal networks with your laptop.

All relationships have flesh and blood, not keys and a screen.

LinkedIn is the greatest tool ever created for professional networking, so use it to the max. But it's just a tool. You've got to get off your butt, turn off your laptop and go out and meet people.

#350:
When employees unionize, it's almost always NOT about the money.

When you work your employees 13 days straight with 1 day off; then turn around and lay them off when the business tanks; keep them in the dark; cut their benefits; then demand their total loyalty and commitment in a work environment populated with Nazi supervisors...you can't be surprised when they reach out for just a tiny bit of third party representation. Can you?

#351:

There are always great HR jobs available, despite the economy. To find them, stand in the bright lights where recruiters and headhunters can find you. They seldom search in the dark alleys. Join SHRM and the chapter in your city. Get access to every HR directory you can find. Update your LinkedIn profile. Ask yourself who you would call first if you were a recruiter looking for YOU. Then take steps to become that person.

#352:
Some HR jobs SUCK. All don't, but some just do. Being in a suck-y HR job isn't your fault. But, staying in a one is. This kind of HR job can control your time and your paycheck, but not your future, unless you let it. There's nothing wrong with keeping an HR job that pays the bills. However, if it limits your true potential, you won't be happy in it for long.

#353:
Approach every so-called disaster, screw-up, mistake, error or embarrassment with the question: 'In five years, will this matter?' Time heals almost everything. Give it time.

#354:
You don't have to win every argument with your boss, your employees, your colleagues or your clients. Know when to agree to disagree.

#355:
When in doubt about what action to take to move things forward, just take the NEXT OBVIOUS *small* STEP.

#356:
Put yourself out there. It's impossible
to maximize your full potential in HR when you stay in
your comfort zone. When you put yourself out there
FULLY and AUTHENTICALLY, the best opportunities find you. You know it's time to leave your
comfort zone when:

- *You hate going to your job in the morning*
- *You're more focused on surviving than thriving*
- *You'd rather keep the boss happy than do your best work*
- *You've lost confidence in the people you work with*
- *You've lost your commitment to the company*
- *You've lost confidence in yourself.*

#357:
CHAOS PRESENTS OPPORTUNITIES. When a
company reorganizes, or a key employee resigns or a
company crisis creates panic among the masses, THIS
IS YOUR TIME TO ACT. Emergencies need answers. Instead of joining those who are grousing,
stalling and waiting for someone else to lead them out
of the wilderness. Step up and ask yourself: "What opportunities are being revealed in this situation that I can
take advantage of to make a positive difference?

#358:
Trust your gut on conversations and relationships. If your brain and your gut disagree, go
with your gut. Your intuition is smarter than
you are and often knows something you don't.

#359:
BOLD actions stand out.

Everyone admires the bold, courageous and daring. No one honors the fainthearted, shy and timid. Fear is a predominant emotion in most large organizations

Fear of getting fired,
Fear of not being promoted,
Fear of making a big mistake,
Fear of showing bad judgment,
Fear of failing to reach targets,
Fear of losing superstar performers,
Or fear of getting a bad reputation.

As an HR professional, taking bold actions and acting with courage and strength...despite your inner fears...marks you as a leader and creates followers.

#360:

Be willing to let go of the old in order to create something new. Regularly upgrade your computer, printer, clothing, car, toxic relationships and underperforming staff. It will keep you alive, vibrant and glowing.

#361:

Change your personal focus from "me" to "you." Put client needs ahead of your own. This tiny mindset shift can single-handedly turn around your HR career. Doing this allows you to stand out in the minds, hearts and checkbooks of your clients.

#362:
Share the credit.

As an HR leader, your greatest satisfaction should come from seeing the people on your team succeed. If your HR team has received recognition from the CEO, be proud, step away and let everyone walk around with the trophy. If you've organized a group that has successfully delivered an innovative new HR program in your organization, stand back and let the group enjoy the thank you's. If your HR team solves a tough client problem, take everyone out to lunch. Let everyone laugh. Let your team glow in the feeling of successfully accomplishing a team goal. Be enthusiastic for them. Share the credit and experience the camaraderie. Your reward will be immense respect and long-lasting relationships.

#363:
THE ASSET WORKING FOR YOU 24 HOURS A DAY. You can create ONE asset that will keep working for you 24 hours a day with all the people who come in contact with you. And, that asset is your REPUTATION. Your success in HR depends on the trust you gain, the assurance you create, the confidence in your judgment, and the personality that you clients see in you. All of this makes up your reputation. However, work on your character too, because your character is what you really are, while your reputation is merely what others think you are.

#364:
A formula for managing your time worth $25,000.

True story. In the 1920s, a man approached JP Morgan, founder of the investment firm that bears his name, and held up an envelope. He said, "Sir, in my hand I hold a GUARANTEED formula for success, which I will gladly sell you for $25,000." "Sir," JP Morgan replied, "I do not know what is in the envelope. However if you show me, and I like it, I give you my word as a gentleman that I will pay you what you ask." The man agreed to those terms, and handed over the envelope. JP Morgan opened it, and extracted a single sheet of paper. He gave it one look, a mere glance, and then handed the piece of paper back. And, then paid him the agreed-upon $25,000. The paper said:

(1) Every morning, write out a list of the 6 MOST IMPORTANT things that need to be done that day.

(2) Do them...in the EXACT order of their importance.

#365:
A simple HR time management memory aid in 12 words:
Do one thing at a time
Most important thing first
Start now.

#366:

Don't quit, you're closer than you think. The temptation to quit will be greatest just before you are about to succeed. Almost nothing works the first time it's attempted. Just because what you're doing does not seem to be working, doesn't mean it won't work. It just means that it might not work the way you're doing it. If it was easy, everyone would be doing it, and you wouldn't have this opportunity.

#367:
Do Not Seek Praise.
Seek Criticism.

It's easy to get approval if you ask enough people, or if you ask those likely to tell you what you want to hear. If, instead of seeking approval, you ask, "What's wrong with it? How can I make it better?" you are more likely to get a truthful and critical answer that can improve on your idea.

#368:

Wrap your arms around the top performing 20% of your employees – and never let them leave because they feel unappreciated. Blow them away with how hard you're willing to commit to them, support them, and with your desire to meet their personal & professional needs.

#369:

The SINGLE MOST POWERFUL TOOL for closing the deal on top-notch job candidates is to have your CEO to call them up and ask them to join the organization. A passionate and personalized call from the top dog in your company will impress job candidates, almost without exception.

#370:

The SECOND MOST SUCCESSFUL CLOSING TOOL is having their new prospective team members call and ask the candidate directly to join their team. Personal expressions of peer support directed at your potential new hires are compelling.

#371 - #378:
Eight Strategies for Keeping Your Key Employees
1. Make sure they have a great leader as a boss.
2. Give them an economic stake – equity or stock options.
3. Offer them help in getting around anything or anyone that gets in the way of their creativity, success or productivity.
4. Create an entrepreneurial environment which stimulates them without becoming adversarial or territorial.
5. Give them the BEST technology, software, or labor saving device at your disposal.
6. Challenge them to produce FAR MORE than they currently are producing -- they need challenges to keep them excited and committed.
7. Eliminate the traditional power structure, reduce politics and reduce levels between them and upper management.
8. Ensure they have visibility to the CEO and the senior leadership team.

#379:
Don't Practice False Kindness.

According to Jack Welch: The worst kind of manager is the one who practices false kindness. In his words: *"I often tell people: You think you're a nice and kind manager? Well guess what? You won't be there someday. You'll be promoted. Or you'll retire. And a new manager will come in and look at your employee and say 'Hey, you're not all that good.' And, all of a sudden, this is employee is now fifty-three or fifty-five without many options in life. And now you're going to tell him, 'Go home?' How is that kind? It isn't. In fact, you're the cruelest kind of manager because you're NOT STRAIGHT WITH PEOPLE!"*

#380:
How to Ace Performance Reviews

- Document and do your own self-appraisals monthly.
- Check in with your boss regularly for feedback and to ensure you're working on the right priorities. Things change quickly.
- Connect your contributions to the business priorities.
- Quantify your contributions.
- Clearly exceed expectations.
- Make sure you have delivered on at least one BIG game-changing, power project that clearly differentiates you from the rest of your peers.

#381:
How to make the HR job market come

to you: Build strong relationships. That's #1, hands down. The best HR job opportunities are rarely published. They are shared in the "hidden" marketplace, passed along quietly from person to person, from search committee to executive recruiter. The only way to tap into this stream of career-building job possibilities is to develop your network of relationships with people who trust you and respect your professionalism. Do what you can to build your recognizability factor in your community, your region, your industry, and with your peers. Network. Speak. Publish. Create innovative HR programs that capture the attention of the media. Work with your government affairs office to help your company take a leadership role in legislation. No matter what the economy is doing, there are always fabulous HR jobs that need to be filled.

#382 - #393:
12 Golden Rules for Managing
Any HR Project Successfully

Rule #1 – Get alignment. Stakeholders and team members must agree on goals and expectations.

Rule #2 -- Build an excellent team. The team must get smart quickly and remain committed to the project's objective…despite all obstacles.

Rule #3 -- Develop a practical, doable plan. Make sure the game plan get communicated to everyone.

Rule #4 -- Make sure you have the resources. Line up the talent, budget and people's time to do the job. Be prepared to negotiate and renegotiate these as needed.

Rule #5-- Have a realistic timetable. The fastest way to lose credibility is to change your timetable without a good reason.

Rule #6 -- Define the scope. Don't bite off more than you can chew. Be clear on what's NOT in scope.

Rule #7 -- People count. HR projects are mostly about people. Flex to meet their needs while staying focused.

Rule #8 -- Get and maintain formal support from managers and all stakeholders. Make the approval process and winning their support a formal event.

Rule #9 -- Be prepared for changes and surprises. Have contingencies.

Rule #10 – Over-communicate. Keep people informed through emails, voicemails and project updates.

Rule #11 -- Think outside of the box. 'Nuff said.

Rule #12 -- Be the leader as well as the manager. Be ruthless on planning, tracking and measuring the project's progress. What gets measured gets done.

#394 - #403:
10 Unmistakable, Tell-Tale Clues That An HR Layoff May Soon Be Coming

Many times we can get so busy as HR pros, we ignore some of the signs that the ax is about to fall. If at least four of the items on this list have taken place, rest assured that layoffs will be following shortly. It's just a matter of time.

1. Company sales and profits are in the toilet.
2. A hiring freeze has just been announced.
3. Pay raises have been deferred for six months or eliminated until further notice.
4. Strict limitations have been placed on travel — especially "non-essential" travel.
5. Monthly expense books are getting scrutinized more or require more approvals.
6. Top HR executives are unavailable, stressed out, distracted or working longer hours than usual.
7. Other executives are canceling routine meetings and spending more time behind closed-doors.
8. Training programs and department training budgets have been cut or eliminated altogether.
9. A merger or acquisition has recently taken place resulting in redundant positions.
10. The buzz and rumors about layoffs is pervasive and off the charts.

#404:

You must always be looking.

Even if you already have a great HR job, if you don't have a plan for getting your next HR gig all lined up, right here, right now, at this very moment, then you're an idiot. Things change in an instant. You are one re-org away from being on the street. You are just one job elimination away from being handed your pink slip. You can be fairly sure that your current HR job is probably not your last. If you go to work tomorrow morning unprepared to leave that afternoon, then you have your head in the sand. Always be mindful of the possibility that today could be your final day at your company.

#405:

Loyalty is for your family.

This is one of the most brutal lessons you'll ever learn if you want outrageous success in HR. But it needs to be said, so here goes. Many companies try to foster a family environment by attempting to create *unconditional* loyalty to the organization. And, it would be great if this loyalty were truly a two-way street and was sustainable. It isn't. And, you and I both know it can't be, if companies want to be competitive. Some HR jobs are removed in an instant, without notice, if the company concludes that that role doesn't help enhance the P&L – even though that family member was loyal. Whether you or I agree with the principle of this doesn't matter. *What matters is that it happens, and you shouldn't let things get to that point.* By being too loyal to your company, you wind up being disloyal to those who matter most – your immediate family.

#406 - #413:
Eight Actions You Can Take To Avoid Getting Laid Off During Tough Times

Thousands of HR professionals are fired, laid off or downsized every year. In a few cases, entire HR departments are wiped out when times are tough. While nothing can guarantee that you or your department won't be next, here's what you can do to stay ahead of the game.

1. Make yourself indispensable.

This is THE big one. Becoming indispensable occurs by acting like an owner in your company and relentlessly asking yourself one simple question: *How can I add MORE value?* Consistently taking action on this question makes it tougher for your boss (and the organization) to carry on without you. Here are four specific steps you can take towards being viewed as indispensable:

- *Go above and beyond your job responsibilities.* During tough times, just doing your own job well simply isn't good enough. You must add more value by going the extra mile and doing more than what's expected. This could include showing you're a team player by multi-tasking, taking on key projects that no one else has time to do or by volunteering to assume the work of someone who has been laid off.

- *Help improve profits.* During business downturns, senior managers are terrified about losing any HR folks who can help make or save money for the organization...because so many HR people DON'T focus enough time in this area. This presents a great opportunity for you to separate yourself from the rest of the pack. Make a list of all the HR programs, external consultants and HR administrative processes you have accountability for. Then, come up with quantifiable ways to enhance their impact (get more for less)....or streamline them (get them done in less time), minimize their cost, eliminate them or defer their cost until a later date. With the help of your Finance department, calculate the dollar value of any improvements you can make in these areas and present these as profit-enhancement suggestions to your organization.

- *Become the #1 go-to person" for a key HR initiative.* Examples here include being a key player during an upcoming labor contract negotiations or the HR leader supporting a revenue producing group like Sales. However, watch the scope of your job. The narrower the focus of your HR role, the easier it will be to whack your job if some of your work can be eliminated or outsourced. So, if you are an HR specialist, this is the time to be very open to key projects assigned to you outside of your area of expertise.

- *Don't major in minor things.* Become ruthless about how you manage your time. Free up your calendar to work on those things your boss or clients consider most important. Eliminate, delegate, outsource and automate as many of your routine, administrative HR activities as possible to create the time and space to showcase your accomplishments to the key decision-makers in your organization. *Examples:* Reduce update meetings that consume time and ask people to update by email instead; Eliminate or streamline any HR reports that nobody reads; Cut back on the number of people that need to approve office supplies, travel arrangements, or software upgrades in your department.

2. Put in the face time.

Despite being awesome at what you do, you can be eliminated during tough times if you're not on the radar screen. Hate to say it, but you're vulnerable if you're taking full advantage of your company's flextime or telecommuting program by working at home. Or, if you're located in a remote site far away from company headquarters.

However, this doesn't mean you shouldn't work remotely.

It just means that if you are, make sure that "out of sight" doesn't mean "out of mind." During tough times, if the key decision makers don't see you, know who are, or feel you don't share their passion for the business, you become very easy to let go.

3. Talk up your contributions.

Great accomplishments aren't enough. You must publicize what you do. There is extensive advice throughout this book about promoting yourself without coming across like a jerk. All that advice especially applies here.

Talk up your contributions to your manager and even to your manager's manager. Provide frequent updates on what you're working on. Don't wait for performance review time to let others know about your accomplishments. It may be too late then.

4. Make sure you're clicking with your boss.

Your hard work, your track record and experience will mean nothing if your job is on the line and your boss hates your guts.

Look for ways to help out, pinch hit, step in or be a sounding board for your boss on work she doesn't like to do. Bring the boss new ideas that make her life easier. If she is working on a restructuring plan and asks for ideas, give her a few good ones. Do some of the heavy lifting yourself.

5. Make sure you're clicking with your clients.

Reach out to your HR clients and ask them for feedback. When rumors about layoffs are in the air, unaddressed client complaints become magnified and can turn into the rationale for your termination. Check in with your clients often and get feedback on how well you are supporting and delivering against their priorities and key initiatives.

6. Have lots of power lunches.

Take a different one of your mentors or advisors to lunch every week. Use these as power lunches where you try pick their brains while trying to keep ketchup off your chin.

With 4 lunches per month, that's 48 more opportunities a year to have lunch to get coaching, build your skills, or gain some wisdom that will help give you the edge if downsizing should occur.

Tough times are the perfect opportunity to forge new connections and deepen long-standing relationships — both inside and outside of your organization. One caution: If you're about to lose your job, it's too late to start building relationships. You need to dig that well long before you're thirsty. So start now.

7. Form and leverage a mastermind group.

Get together with your staff or people in your network to brainstorm opportunities for thriving during difficult times. When several people get together with a blank slate and some good energy, magic can happen. Ask for ideas and you might be surprised by the results. You can build new skills and experiences through the help of a few of your trusted colleagues and professional contacts.

8. Don't whine.

Your attitude matters. Those walking frowning and seemingly pissed off at the organization are always candidates to be shown the door during tough times.

Stay optimistic and flexible when unplanned situations come up. Do a personal attitude check to make sure that you are putting your best foot forward.

Yes, it is tough remaining upbeat and positive when it feels like the bottom is falling out. So remain in contact with your network of professionals, friends and family to help you through the rough spots.

#414:

Absolutely Convinced You're About To Get Laid Off Your HR Job? Then Follow These Steps BEFORE It Happens...

Sometimes, no matter what you've done, the decision has been made. It's too late and there's nothing you can do about it. If that's the case, it's time to get proactive and take action before the ax falls.

Step 1:   Accept the fact that your job may not be safe.

Fact the facts. No matter what your HR position is in the company, nobody is indispensable. But don't space out. If management has not yet selected who will be let go, you want to improve your odds of being the one retained. So stay calm, keep your head down and continue to focus on your job.

However, prepare for the worst. If you're not let go, that's great. But if you are, you'll feel better and gain greater control over your destiny if you start preparing in advance.

Step 2:   Start discreetly reaching out to your network.

Outplacement experts rightfully preach that networking is the best way to find another job. So get a head start. Use the time wisely while you still have a job. Start quietly checking in with your colleagues, vendors, clients, or peers at other companies. Set up breakfast and lunch meetings with as many of these folks as possible. Your only objective at this point is to re-connect and line up these relationships so that you'll feel more comfortable calling on them later should the ax fall.

Step 3: Prepare your spouse or significant other.

As tough as it may be to discuss your fears, you need to lay it on the line with your partner about your current job situation. Trying to protect him or her from possible bad news, while admirable, may well backfire if your partner feels that you have intentionally kept them in the dark.

Step 4: Investigate your company's severance policy.

Being in HR, you know that most companies don't disclose or publish any printed information on severance policies. But most use a formula based on rank and years of service. Others just wing it as they go along. So, finding out what you will be paid upon termination can require some digging. Your best source of information will be your trusted peers in HR or other employees who have been recently laid off. As you gather information, it's important to not only find out the amount of severance you can reasonably expect, but also:

- Does the company make lump-sum severance payments or continue employees on the payroll? Will your severance payments stop if you find another job?
- Will they extend your insurance benefits?
- Do they provide outplacement assistance?
- Do they offer alternatives to severance? Some companies have recently started to offer employees leave of absence packages as an alternative to termination.

Step 5: Begin taking possession of your personal belongings, personal files and e-mail addresses.

If you are let go, you could be escorted out on the spot and denied the opportunity to go back to your office to clean out your personal stuff. So, now is the time to sort through your personal files and take them home. Just be careful not to remove anything that could be deemed company property or proprietary in nature.

Since your network is the key to a successful job search, you'll want to be sure that you've got all the telephone numbers and e-mail addresses of your valued contacts for future reference. If this information is maintained on company-owned equipment (such as a PC or PDA) copy those files to a CD and take it home. Or copy all pertinent data to your home e-mail account. TIP: Be subtle in your packing activities - you don't want to create the impression that you're expecting to be let go. Although the company may not allow you back in your office after being dismissed, they will return your personal belongings so don't feel the need to take down personal photos quite yet. But, consider removing anything you consider personal or valuable in a non-obvious manner.

Step 6: Update your resume.

In today's workplace, you should always have an up-to-date resume on your hard drive. You never know when a perfect job opportunity might surface. So don't let an outdated resume prevent you from reacting to new opportunities in a timely manner.

Step 7: Re-establish ties with executive recruiters.

If you've successfully worked with recruiters in the past, give them a call to touch base. Send them your updated resume and a brief cover letter. Again, start laying the ground work.

Step 8: Investigate job opportunities elsewhere within your company.

In some large companies, one division can be laying people off, while another division thrives and is hiring. If you have skills that might be attractive to other departments or divisions, look into options for transfer.

Step 9: Hold off on long-term financial commitments.

If you have financial concerns, it goes without saying that you should put off buying that new home, undertaking a major remodeling project or purchasing that new car. The last thing you need right now is to be hampered with new monthly payment obligations.

Step 10: Pay off your credit card debt.

With credit card interest rates, the cost of maintaining a monthly credit balance can be staggering. If it's not possible to totally eliminate the debt quickly, investigate ways to consolidate the payments on a card with a lower interest rate.

Creatively increase your savings account. Certain bills such as auto insurance, health clubs, etc. can often be paid in either a lump sum or installment payments. If you normally pay them on an annual basis, this may be a good time to look into monthly or quarterly payments instead. Surprisingly, the borrowing cost on these installment plans can be quite low, providing you with the option of maintaining a higher cushion in your savings account during this critical time period.

Step 11: Use your employee benefits, before you lose them.

In the event of a job loss, your job benefits will most likely be terminated. While you will be given the opportunity to extend your health coverage through COBRA, now is the time to maximize your other benefits.

Personal Days: If you need to take time away from the job, save your vacation days by depleting your personal days first. After termination, you're normally entitled to receive pay for accrued vacation time, while payment for unused personal days or holidays is rare.

Vision Benefits: If you're entitled to a vision care plan, schedule your family's eye exams and purchase of glasses/contact lenses immediately.

Max out your Medical Flexible Spending Account: If you are fortunate enough to participate in a section 125-reimbursement account, you can claim all eligible expenses (prescription drug costs, eye care, unreimbursed medical deductibles, etc.) incurred through your date of termination, even if you have not yet fully contributed to the plan. So, do what you can now to maximize those reimbursable expenses – schedule check-ups, order all needed prescriptions, and get your family in tip-top medical shape at an unbeatable price!

Dependent Care: If your child is enrolled in a company-sponsored childcare program, you should investigate the company's policy regarding your right to continue participating in that program following your termination. If that is not an option, begin to collect data on suitable childcare services in your area.

Other benefits: Is your company affiliated with a work-life service that provides helpful information about eldercare, referrals to summer camps, or daycare providers? How about the little perks – like membership at Sam's Club? Take advantage of these services while you are still eligible.

Layoffs are a fact of life. Even though you should always stay positive and focus on the best, you should also get your head out of the sand and prepare for the worse. You don't want to get caught flat-footed. Hopefully, these steps will help prepare you if you're about to be terminated.

#415 - #421:

7 Reasons You're NOT Getting HR Job Offers ...What Your Interviewers Know, But Aren't Telling You!

The simplest way to find out why you're getting job interviews but no offers is to just call up the people you interviewed with and get direct feedback from them. Easy to do, right? Yes, it is...

...BUT, DON'T COUNT ON IT HAPPENING ANYTIME SOON!

Here's why:

One, they're too busy.

Two, they expect you to (of course) disagree with their assessment and they have absolutely no interest in having this to escalate into a full-blown verbal brawl.

And three, they don't want to risk a lawsuit by saying the wrong thing.

Think about it. Who can blame them?

So, in lieu of getting direct feedback from your interviewers, here are seven REAL reasons you're not getting offers – and what to do about it...

1. There's nothing special about you.

I'm sorry but you're just like every other HR pro they've interviewed. There's no difference between you and the last three "result-oriented HR generalists" they've talked with. Nothing distinguishes you from the rest of the flock.

Solution: Make a list of the things you've done that set you apart from others and ways you can solve their HR, employee engagement, retention, cost management or business problems...and be prepared to talk about them in your interviews. Rehearse communicating this information over and over until you are so good at it that you exude the confidence that shows that you know your stuff.

Also, cut out all the HR jargon, psychobabble and buzzwords. Use plain speak. Envision interviewing with your grandmother. Yes, it may be tough to avoid saying: "I'm strategic," but try it.

2. You're lazy.

You didn't do enough homework. Or, you got so busy you didn't have enough time to prepare the way you wanted. And, it showed. So, what should you be preparing for? In a word: EVERYTHING.

Solution: Find out as much about the position as you can so you can decide if you even want it and so you can position yourself as the best fit for the job. Knowing all you can about the company will help you decide if you like its direction and share its values.

Plus, when it comes to the all important "Do you have any questions for us?" portion of the interview, all this preparation will ensure that you have plenty of material to cover.

Also, to prove that you're a well-prepared, smart, no-nonsense HR professional from the get-go, be ready to ask well-thought-out, specific questions. Write them out in advance, so that you don't forget them under pressure. Be prepared to interview the interviewer. Sometimes all it takes to get the hiring manager's attention AND TO SET YOURSELF APART FROM OTHER CANDIDATES is ASKING THE RIGHT QUESTION or, better still, the right question that no one else has asked.

I know all of this isn't glamorous and you probably know a lot of this already, but the key here is EXECUTION! PRACTICE YOUR PITCH IN FRONT OF THE MIRROR, to get connected to it and believe in it. This will allow you to feel confident, comfortable in your own skin.

3. You're boring as hell.

Surveys of hiring managers and HR leaders show that the number one trait that HR job seekers lack is high energy, enthusiasm, passion for the job. The bottom line is that most HR folks want to be around other people who are upbeat, exciting and at the very least, energetic.

The perception is that high energy HR people are on the ball and exude confidence. Low energy people are lazy, unmotivated and no fun. Whether this is true or not doesn't matter. What matters is that you address this perception.

Solution: Do a gut check to determine how you come across. And I'm not just talking about the live interview where your handshake needs to be strong and secure (ladies included) and your voice confident and strong.

During your phone interview, your energy is even more important because no one can see the bright expression of excitement that is hidden by technology. The only way to portray confidence and high energy on the phone is to have the proper inflection, tonality and great volume. With blue tooth and other type headsets, it's more and more important to speak up.

If you're not excited about what you have to offer, why should anyone else be? And please get some honest feedback from a trusted colleague about how you sound. Do an autopsy of your interviews and networking exchanges. Do you come across on paper (and in person) as someone who is blah, boring, flat, disengaged and lethargic?

If you think that you might, how about injecting some passion, energy, drive, motivation, determination, and inspiration into the wonderful product - YOU!

3. You're not memorable.

The reason you're not memorable is that you lack a compelling story that the interviewer can relate to. There's an old saying: "stories sell and facts tell."

Interesting stories create emotions and get people connected. People can relate personally to stories and the more you know about the company and person that you are interviewing with, **the better you can use a story drawn from your own experiences to get that person to relate to what you are talking about.**

And getting personally and emotionally to your interviewers is the differentiator you need.

Solution: A powerful way to find your own stories is to call up former colleagues, employees and bosses just shoot the breeze with them. Write down all the wonderful, "remember when" stories as well as the stories of your HR successes and challenges that make you unique, interesting, personable and different.

If you've spent years in HR, you may need other people to jog your memory. If you can give your story personality and feeling, then you will gain instant rapport with anyone you talk to.

Stories are an instant differentiator. Find a couple that are uniquely yours, then use them.

4. You don't talk enough about money in your interviews.

In tough times, EVERYONE is talking money. Around kitchen tables everywhere, most families are discussing how to SAVE money or how to MAKE more money.

The same is true in the companies you're interviewing with. It is important to recognize that as an HR professional, you are an investment. The hiring company invests in you with the expectation that you will produce returns on that investment. What types of returns? Most employers are seeking HR folks who have the proven ability to SOLVE a challenging problem, to help them MAKE money, to help them SAVE money, or to help them INCREASE efficiency and productivity.

Solution: Keep in mind that employers are looking for "experts" and "solution providers" that can address THEIR issues. By taking time to describe in quantifiable terms the results you have delivered against, you can easily set yourself apart from the masses of the HR folks who are just emphasizing the soft stuff.

5. You're bitter and it comes through in your interviews.

Yes, you're still ticked off that you were fired, laid off or forced out. And try as you might, you couldn't resist a little subtle dig at your boss or your former company. And deep down inside it felt good to vent a little bit. But wrong time, wrong place. Not cool.

Nobody wants to hire a whiner Nobody owes you a job. When unemployment is high and you find yourself in a competitive job market, it is easy to get discouraged. It's a fact that right now there are more and more people competing for fewer and fewer HR jobs.

Solution: Focus on the positive in your interviews. Take the high road, even if you feel you've been screwed over by your last employer. Keep in mind that there are still great HR jobs to be found. Even in the toughest economic climates, companies are still hiring and HR job seekers are landing jobs on a daily basis.

7. They're just not that into you.

They don't like you. You're not what they want. You just didn't click with them. The chemistry just wasn't there. Why? Who knows? Have you ever talked to someone that makes you say, "hey, this doesn't feel right"?

Well how do you know if someone isn't saying that about you? Here's the best way to tell. If you have anything to hide, have covered something up, or speak in half truths or your resume doesn't match what you say – these are dead giveaways.

If any of those things are true, people will say to themselves, "this doesn't feel right." The biggest lies we tell are the ones we tell ourselves (think of your small kids who will swear they didn't take the last pizza slice, all the while covered in pizza sauce). If this is you...no job, guaranteed!

Solution: You don't have to be perfect and convey that you have no problems. In fact the only people with no problems are, well, dead people. Just be honest and be consistent.

There you have it, seven reasons why they're NOT SHOWING YOU'RE THE MONEY. So consider this a wakeup call...and also a terrific opportunity to truly differentiate yourself and win that offer!

#422 - #425
4 New Rules for Winning in HR

...But Only If You're Female, Black, Latino, Asian, Native American, Gay, Straight, Young, Old, Disabled or Not...or White Male

New Rule #1: Stop complaining about your company's commitment to diversity and inclusion, if you're not walking the talk yourself.

You're an idiot with no credibility if you're whining about your company's progress on D&I but doing nothing to move it forward yourself. Let me illustrate...

Years ago, at a meeting of our African American Council at our division of Pepsi, the leaders were complaining that the company's progress on inclusion wasn't moving fast enough. Our executive sponsor, who was a white male CFO in the company, asked us out of curiosity to share the names of three people we were all personally mentoring. A few had none. Most had at least one. With a couple of exceptions, all the mentees named were the exact race and gender as we were.

He then challenged us by saying: *"It's easy to complain. But as the senior African American leaders in this company, you're not walking the talk either. There's no way things will change around here if you're only mentoring people just like you. Here's what I'd propose. Why don't you set a personal objective that you will mentor 3 people over the next six months who are all different (more diverse than you are). And I'll do the same thing, because frankly I need to walk the talk better too."*

At a follow up meeting six months later, we all excitedly reported back on our progress. Doing this was so insightful and developmental for us personally that we all continued our mentoring relationships well beyond the six months we committed to. In addition, we all cascaded this down to our teams. This simple little initiative shortly spread throughout the organization and was a very positive step forward in driving inclusion in the company.

Stop listening to what folks say, but instead to watch what they do. It's easy to complain about your workplace. But what are you doing about it?

As an HR professional, you lose the right to complain about inclusion, if you're not walking the talk yourself. Not sure where to start? Well, are there 3 people different than you, who could learn from your experience, who you can start mentoring...tomorrow?

New HR Rule #2: Don't bury who you really are.

Lots of HR people walk on eggshells these days. They bury who they really are. They do this because they believe their organizations don't really value their uniqueness. Or, they fear they'll get biased treatment. And in many cases, they're right.

I've talked about this in elsewhere in this book, but let me reiterate: To excel, you must be able to bring your "whole" real self to work. Here's why: unless you're in a Broadway play, it's too confusing and exhausting to play one role by day, be yourself at night and sustain your "A" game. And you need to tap into every ounce of energy you have if you're going to compete with the best and brightest in your organization every day.

At one time, many of us were trained to sanitize our resumes, removing any trace of our ethnicity, sexual orientation or cultural heritage for fear that we wouldn't be interviewed.

Today, that's still a very real risk in many organizations, though increasingly less so. But, if you're going to find a place where you can thrive and make an "emotional investment," in the company's success, you're going to need to take a risk – maybe even a big risk. That means feeling comfortable talking about that pick-up basketball game you played in the inner city on weekends instead of golf. It means being comfortable sharing your activities in the Gay Pride events in your town.

I will make no pretense that any of this is easy to do or will be embraced with open arms by everyone. But it's necessary if you want to find organizations that you can embrace fully, feel comfortable in, and passionate about.

New Rule #3: **If you're in the job market, avoid companies that just COUNT HEADS -- they must also make these HEADS COUNT.**

When I first started in HR, the company I joined bragged about their diversity program. While there were no minority or female VPs at the time, they had quite an impressive and diverse group of HR managers. That was one reason I joined them. When I finally made HR manager (at a different company, mind you), 95% of those impressive managers had long gone. Here's why:

- They were treated like dirt.
- There was no mentoring.
- There was no support system.
- There was no encouragement.
- The firm didn't reward developing diverse talent.
- They had no commitment from the top.
- There was no culture of inclusion.

For EEO compliance reasons, that company was only interested in counting heads. If talented diverse people left, they were simply replaced. Those were the old rules.

Here is the new rule: If you want to win in HR, you owe it to yourself to plant your career in an organization that not only <u>counts heads</u>...but <u>makes those heads count.</u> How do you know if that exists? Go up two paragraphs and read through those seven bullets again...and see if the opposite exists.

New HR Rule #4: Don't make it about being black, brown or white -- make it about the GREEN.

Accept the fact that life isn't fair. Fair is something that you pay when you jump in a taxi (i.e. fare). You make your own breaks. Don't worry about why you were hired. You could be hired in HR because the diversity plan calls for bringing in an Asian female. The guy next to you could be hired because he's the CEO's white godson. You were both hired because of your ethnicities. So what? You both got in.

Now that you're in, focus on distinguishing yourself by figuring out ways to help your business generate more of the green stuff. As an HR pro, make building your financial intelligence about your business and delivering value priority one.

Will that eliminate bias and make things fair? Probably not. Your may still feel your mistakes are magnified more than those of others. You may still be misperceived, misinterpreted or even stereotyped on occasion. You may still have to be better adept at building alliances and marketing your accomplishments in order to succeed.

However, you can waste precious time grousing about the unfairness of it all, or you can invest that same time making yourself indispensable. Of course, today no one really is irreplaceable. But by focusing your HR attention on ways to help your organization become more competitive, you can become a valuable, tough-to-replace commodity...the type of commodity no wants to get rid of and that other companies would like to retain...NO MATTER WHO YOU ARE.

#426:
SIDEHUSTLING: How to keep your HR job and make extra income on the side during tough times.

I seriously considered leaving this out of this book.

It's an HR career model that a surprising number of HR pros engage in at some point during their HR careers. It's also a career strategy practically no one in HR talks about. And it is for that reason I decided to include it.

You won't read about this in *Workforce* magazine, *HR Executive* or find it as a featured topic at any SHRM meeting.

What is it?

It's called **sidehustling** and here's how I stumbled on to it.

A buddy of mine who is an HR director in Chicago recently informed me that he was taking an advanced online class on how to sell stuff on eBay.

Totally shocked and just a bit curious, I asked him:

"Why the heck are you wasting time taking a class on eBay when you could be using the time instead to take a class on talent retention, health care cost containment or how to leverage social media in HR? Those are the hot topics right now for HR...wouldn't those be better for your HR career?"

"Sure, but hey," he replied passionately, **"Doing the eBay thing is my side hustle to put a little more cash in my pocket. I**

absolutely love HR to death, but the health care company I work has eliminated merit increases entirely for this year and I can use the extra income. This advanced eBay class is going to help me do that."

He went on to say: "You see, I've been a coin collector since I was in grade school. And, I worked in a coin shop during the summer to help pay for college. Now, I make a nice little side income buying and selling them a couple of evenings a week from home on my laptop on eBay. At one point, I thought about opening up my own coin business full-time as a coin dealer, but it was just too risky and expensive. So, I decided to turn my passion into my sidehustle instead. I've been buying and selling coins at a profit for over four years on eBay — all while keeping my day job in HR. So back to your question...yes, I'm looking at building my skills in HR, but I want to keep my side hustle going too."

After we talked a bit more, it was hard to argue with his logic. And one thing struck me...

More HR pros need a sidehustle.

Let's face it, the economy is at an all time low, the housing and job markets are in the middle of a crisis, credit is hard to find and keep, and many exceptional HR pros are out on the street or having a hard time meeting their monthly financial obligations.

While many search for a better paying job or work towards advancing their HR career right where they are, many others are also choosing to sidehustle.

If you're in HR, a sidehustle may be a great alternative for:

- Earning a few extra bucks on the side.
- Testing and trying out a new business idea.
- Keeping some revenue flowing in if you've lost your job and are in transition.

Here are a few examples of sidehustles people that I know are doing successfully on evenings, weekends or part-time...while balancing the demands of their full-time gig.

- Teaching HR classes at a local university or community college
- Providing a resume-writing service or career coaching.
- Consulting with small businesses
- Writing for blogs, websites, their local newspaper or for national magazines
- Teaching English (Spanish or any another language) to those wanting to learn a second language
- Becoming a paid fund raiser for local charities
- Doing event planning for local organizations
- Buying real estate and renting it out
- Buying stocks that pay annual dividends
- Selling personal photography or art
- Buying and selling collectibles on eBay

Obviously, some of these sidehustles are more risky than others. Some are related to HR. Some aren't. While the people doing them won't become as rich as Oprah, Bill Gates or Lady Gaga, they're finding the extra spare-time income helpful.

While many are choosing <u>not</u> to hide their sidehustles from their full-time employers, they DON'T widely publicize them either.

They don't want their sidehustle to get them fired from their main hustle. So, if asked, they refer to them as their "hobbies" or "spare-time interests," because they don't want to be perceived as not being 100% committed to their organization's success.

So what's your side hustle?

One of the things I do in my spare time is to create websites. I've never called this my sidehustle, but that's exactly what it is. Its fun for me and it creates another revenue stream. Besides sites I create for myself, I've created blogs for local judges, real estate agents and a couple of interior designers.

Over the years, I've learned how to produce these sites quickly in my spare time...without diverting me from my main focus which is my HR work and career. And it's a good change of pace for me, allowing me channel my creative juices into something not related to HR. I've even created a new website about this whole idea of sidehustling...and it includes a ton of sidehustle ideas you may want to consider...check it out at www.SideHustling.com.

From my own experience and talking with others, a good sidehustle will have the following characteristics:

- You like doing it.
- You are pretty good at it.
- **It may be related to your career in HR...but it doesn't have to be.**
- You can generate some quick cash in a short period of time
- **It does not require a huge amount of time away from your HR day job.**
- You focus on one hustle at a time to keep your stress level low.
- **It does not create a conflict of interest situation with your company** *(very important!!)*.
- Start with an easy hustle first.
- Set goals and time frames to get your hustle started.
- **It is ideal if your hustle is an extension of your HR brand.** *For example, if you're an HR generalist, teaching an HR class in the evening at a local university is great for your resume and great for your pocketbook.*
- Your hustle will not get you thrown in jail (*dealing crack, while profitable and possible from your home, is not recommended*)

Sidehustling is only whispered about, but practiced widely...and is a great option for navigating your HR career in uncertain times.

#427 - #431:
5 Simple Life Lessons Every HR Professional Should Embrace

Life Lesson #1:
The Cleaning Lady

During my second month of college, our professor gave us a pop quiz. I was confident that I had nailed this test and breezed through the questions until I read the last one: 'What is the first name of the woman who cleans the school?'

Surely this was some kind of joke. I had passed by the cleaning woman many times. She was short, white-haired and in her 50's, but how would I know her name?

I handed in my paper, and left the last question blank. Just before class ended, someone asked if the last question would count toward our quiz grade.

'Absolutely,' said the professor. 'In your careers, you will meet many people. All are significant. They deserve your attention and care, even if all you do is smile and say 'hello.'

I've never forgotten that lesson. I also learned her name was Olivia.

Life Lesson #2: Pickup in the Rain

One night, at midnight, an older African American woman was standing on the side of the highway in Alabama during a terrible rainstorm. Her car wouldn't start and she desperately needed a ride.

Soaking wet, she decided to flag down the next car. A young white man stopped to help her, clearly something that didn't happen every day in the South during the 1960's. The man took her to safety, helped her get assistance for her car and put her in a taxi.

She left in a big hurry, but wrote down his address and thanked him. Seven days went by and a knock came on the man's door. To his surprise, a giant console color TV was delivered to his home. A special note was attached.

It read: "Thank you so much for assisting me on the highway the other night. The rain drenched not only my clothes, but also my spirits. Then you came along. Because of you, I was able to make it to my dying husband's bedside just before he passed away. Thank you for helping me and unselfishly serving others." -- Sincerely, Mrs. Nat King Cole.

Life Lesson #3: Serving More than Ice Cream

In the days when an ice cream sundae cost much less, a 10-year-old boy entered a hotel coffee shop and sat at a table. A waitress put a glass of water in front of him.

"How much is an ice cream sundae?" he asked.

"Fifty cents," replied the waitress.

The little boy pulled his hand out of his pocket and studied the coins in it.

"Well, how much is a plain dish of ice cream?" he inquired. By now more people were waiting for a table and the waitress was growing impatient.

"Thirty-five cents," she brusquely replied.

The little boy again counted his coins.

"I'll have the plain ice cream," he said.

The waitress brought the ice cream, put the bill on the table and walked away. The boy finished the ice cream, paid the cashier and left. When the waitress came back, she began to cry as she wiped down the table. There, placed neatly beside the empty dish, were two nickels and five pennies.

You see, he couldn't have the sundae, because he had to have enough left to leave her a tip.

Life Lesson #4: The Obstacle in Our Path

In ancient times, a king had a boulder placed on a roadway. Then he hid himself and watched to see if anyone would remove the huge rock. Some of the king's wealthiest merchants and courtiers came by and simply walked around it. Many loudly blamed the King for not keeping the roads clear, but none did anything about getting the stone out of the way.

Then a peasant came along carrying a load of vegetables. Upon approaching the boulder, the peasant laid down his burden and tried to move the stone to the side of the road. After much pushing and straining, he finally succeeded.

After the peasant picked up his load of vegetables, he noticed a purse lying in the road where the boulder had been. The purse contained many gold coins and a note from the King indicating that the gold was for the person who removed the boulder from the roadway.

The peasant learned what few people in the world truly understand: Within every obstacle lies a golden opportunity to improve your current situation.

Life Lesson #5: Giving When It Really Counts

Many years ago, when I worked as a volunteer at a hospital, I got to know a little girl named Liz who was suffering from a rare & serious disease. Her only chance of recovery appeared to be a blood transfusion from her 5-year old brother, who had miraculously survived the same disease and had developed the antibodies needed to combat the illness.

The doctor explained the situation to her little brother, and asked the little boy if he would be willing to give his blood to his sister. I saw him hesitate for only a moment before taking a deep breath and saying, "Yes I'll do it if it will save her."

As the transfusion progressed, he lay in bed next to his sister and smiled, as we all did, seeing the color returning to her cheek. Then his face grew pale and his smile faded. He looked up at the doctor and asked with a trembling voice, "Will I start to die right away?"

Being young, the little boy had misunderstood the doctor; he thought he was going to have to give his sister all of his blood in order to save her...but he had chosen to save her anyway.

Five simple life lessons. What do they mean for you in HR?

Here are five things you should take away:

1) In our HR careers, we will meet many people. <u>All are significant</u>. They all deserve our attention and care, even if all you do is smile and say "hello."

2) As HR professionals, we all have a unique opportunity and platform for <u>serving others</u>. Never underestimate it. Even our smallest gestures that show we care can affect others' lives profoundly.

3) Always <u>remember your team members who serve you</u>, even in the smallest way. Never take them for granted, even if they take you for granted!

4) Within every obstacle lies a_golden op-portunity_ to improve your current situation and to DRAMATICALLY move your HR career forward.

5) "You can't have a perfect day in HR without doing something for someone who will never be able to repay you." So give when it counts...and give without counting. Just give...if you want to make a real difference in someone's job, their career or their life.

This is what attaining awesome success in HR is REALLY all about. Isn't it?

Onward!

More HR Career Success Resources
by Alan Collins

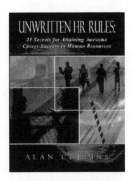

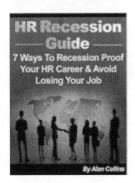

THE BRYAN A. COLLINS SCHOLARSHIP PROGRAM

 The Bryan A. Collins Memorial Scholarship Program awards scholarship grants every year to minority students who demonstrate excellence in pursuit of their college degrees. Students selected for this scholarship must embody the values embraced by the late Bryan A. Collins -- great with people, great at academics and great in extra-curricular leadership activities.

Bryan Collins was a rising star and well-respected student leader at Tennessee State University. Bryan received his B.S. degree in Biology from TSU in May 2005. At the time of his passing, he was enrolled in the Masters program in physical therapy and anxiously looking forward to commencing his doctoral studies. On campus, he was a leader in the Kappa Alpha Psi fraternity, served on the Civic Committee, the Community Service Committee and help set strategic direction as a Board Member of the fraternity.

In addition, he found much success outside the classroom. He was voted Mr. Tennessee State first runner-up, was involved in the Student Union Board of Governors, was a founding member of the Generation of Educated Men and worked closely with the Tennessee State University dean of admissions and records.

Bryan found comfort and relaxation in sports, music, movies, video games, friends, good parties and just spending time with his family relaxing at home.

The key contributors to Bryan's scholarship program include the PepsiCo Foundation, Pamela Hewitt & Warren Lawson of Chicago, the Motorola Foundation and many other organizations and individuals.

Additional details about Bryan, the scholarship program and how to contribute can be found at the scholarship website at: www.BryanCollinsScholarship.org.

ABOUT THE AUTHOR

Alan Collins is President of Success in HR, and author of the best-seller, *Unwritten HR Rules.*

He was formerly Vice President of Human Resources at PepsiCo where he led HR initiatives for their Quaker Oats, Gatorade and Tropicana businesses. With 25 years as an HR executive and professional, Alan's corporate and operating human resources experience is extensive. While at PepsiCo, he led a team of 60 HR directors, managers and professionals spread across 21 different locations in North America, where he was accountable for their performance, careers and success. He and his team provided HR strategic and executional oversight for a workforce of over 7000 employees supporting $8 billion in sales. Alan also served as the HR M&A lead in integrating new acquisitions as well as divesting existing businesses; and he provided HR leadership for one of the largest change initiatives in the history of the Pepsi organization. He also served as co-leader of the Quaker-Tropicana-Gatorade African American Network and was selected as a PepsiCo executive member of the prestigious Executive Leadership Council, based in Washington D.C.

He has been a featured speaker at various HR conferences and seminars throughout the U.S. including the National Conference for the Society for Human Resources Management (SHRM).

He has written over 100 articles and white papers on HR and his perspectives have been featured in various human resources national publications including *HR Executive, HRM Today, Linked:HR,* and *Personal Branding.* He has also taught at various Chicago-area universities.

He received his BS and MS degrees in Industrial Relations from Purdue. More about Alan and his works can be accessed at: www.SuccessInHR.com. He resides in Chicago.

Made in the USA
Lexington, KY
16 April 2012